Seducing CELEBRITIES

One Meal at a Time

Seducing
CELEBRITIES

One Meal at a Time

Thaao Penghlis

Brick Tower Press
Habent Sua Fata Libelli

Brick Tower Press
Manhanset House
Dering Harbor, New York 11965-0342
Tel: 212-427-7139
bricktower@aol.com · www.BrickTowerPress.com

Library of Congress Cataloging-in-Publication Data
Penghlis, Thaao.
Seducing Celebrities, One Meal at a Time

978-1-899694-57-0, Hardcover
978-1-899694-19-8, Trade Paper

1. Cooking—General 2. Biography—Rich & Famous 3. Biography &
Autobiography—Entertainment and Performing Arts—General I. Title:
Seducing Celebrities. II. Title.

March 2024

I'd like to acknowledge and thank my manager Alan Morell who planted the seed for this book when we first met for lunch at Shutters in Santa Monica.

To my dear mother Eva who was able in times of struggle to make the table our family shared, rich in the expressions of our heritage.

To the Kastellorizian Society in Sydney who rewarded me with their Culture and Cuisine that I am still influenced by today; to my sisters Pauline and Connie for exchanging their recipes when I needed them; my cousins Christianne and George Antonas, and my sister-in-law Helen Pengly for always celebrating me with their magnificent dinners so wonderfully executed when I was in Sydney.

To Denise George who helped me put this book together, and to a special soul, Dr. Christine Dumas, for her constant belief and support on encouraging me that *Seducing Celebrities* was a unique and timely book. She is truly a treasure.

A special thank you to John Colby and his team for making my stories and recipes come alive.

Thanks also to Daphne Valentina for her wonderful ideas on Greek Cuisine.

A special thanks to Valorie Massalas for always taking notes when I was experimenting in new types of cuisine.

And finally, to Sheri Anderson to whom I dedicate this book for teaching me the meaning of the word.

CONTENTS

INTRODUCTION

WHEN I LOOK AT my life thus far, nutrition has always been a priority. In my early years when I could afford only a tin of Ravioli for dinner, I promised myself that when success came my way this unnourished lifestyle would change. And so it did. I discovered that food has its own mysteries just like the journey of life; by learning to unravel its nutritional secrets you can discover how it best serves the self and allows you to influence others by the way you live.

I learned from my Greek heritage that ancient adage "Nothing in excess and know thyself." It set the pattern of discovery in my desires and curbed those that did not reward my being. By applying these methods continually through the years my body was able to heal the effects of pressure on itself quickly, and by doing so my temperament was rewarded.

By investigating the enormous rewards that nutrition brings "knowledge through intuition, smell and taste," you discover your body's secrets by the way you feed it and how it feeds you back. With so many choices, we are blessed through its abundance and variety. For me food is the magic of our universe. It is also the great seductress. The aroma, the presentation, the touch, taste and texture, bring atmosphere by the cuisine chosen.

That all translates to the brain a message that says, "This feast of the senses makes me feel loved."

I always believed that people's behavior is illuminated by the way a table is presented. It becomes a watering hole for the guests gathered through the romance of it all and continues through the night by the way they are united in this ritual. And at its core is the nourishment and pleasure the food provides. A Rabbi told me over Greek coffee one afternoon that the secret to health is "For breakfast you eat like a King, for lunch like a Prince and for dinner be a Pauper. And Greek coffee they have discovered is the key to a longer life." Salute to wisdom.

Because of our work ethic so many of us in the last few years are buying prepared food and frozen meals, compromising taste for convenience. I make my own soups and freeze them so when time is short, at least I know where the food came from and how it was prepared. And I know it will nourish me. I finally understood that by mastering the ingredients of a particular recipe I was able to see how doing one thing well could unravel a mystery by incorporating the ingredients I chose into my acting. Somehow understanding one thing well becomes a foundation for all other venues to master.

I have met and worked with many entertainers in my life. The idea of this book came to me one evening while visiting Cuba. I expand on this in the chapter "Finding a seed inside

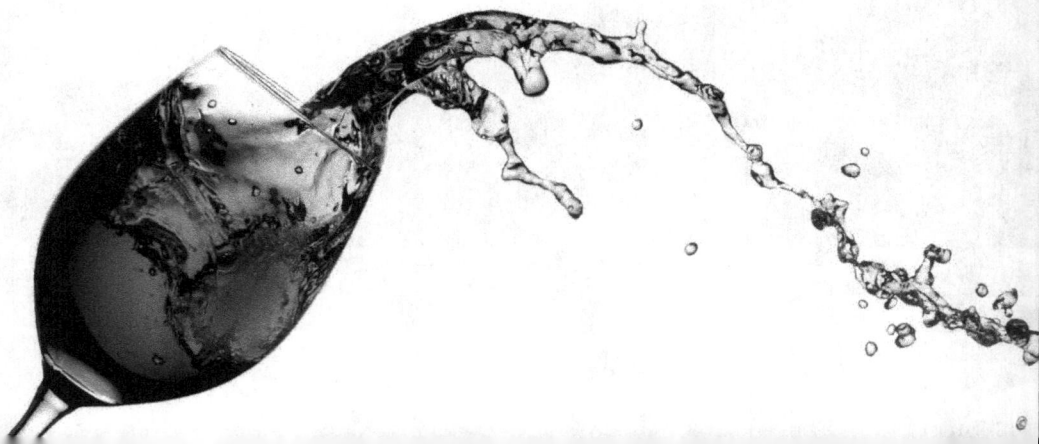

Havana." Also the wonderful actress Doris Roberts came for dinner one evening and wrote me a letter that stated, "An extraordinary cook who takes pleasure in inviting his friends to his home for an evening of great food, wine and interesting conversation. The table is so beautiful that you hate to sit down to mess it up. The food that he cooks takes time, thoughtfulness and knowledge, and he spends hours preparing it. Did I mention the aroma that greets you when you walk into his house?"

Havana and Doris's thoughtful letter inspired me to take those generous comments to a new plateau. With all the celebrities that crossed my path through social means or at work, how would I embrace and seduce them with the cuisine I have discovered through a lifetime of preparation? Through my imagination and experiences I have put together recipes that would resonate with these wonderful talents.

With Jacqueline Kennedy with whom I had afternoon tea in my youth, I would have prepared as she was marrying Onassis, a Greek cuisine: Greek lemon soup, Moussaka and the celebratory cookies "Kourambiedes." George Clooney, for his love of Italy: Branzino fish. Barbara Streisand and Shirley Maclaine: Rack of Lamb, because they love the best in Cuisine. Joan Rivers: Scallops and Vongole, (because it sounds delicate with a vengeance). Omar Sharif: "Lamb Shanks with Couscous" and Champagne with dessert because that's what he always shared when we worked together. And

Elizabeth Taylor: Thai Snapper and a special dessert from my family's heritage, because she reigned supreme.

I am always looking for the next step of fulfillment on this journey I have chosen. Sadly, it seems like culture and cuisine are fading by the choices in people's lifestyles, and our health, joy and longevity are suffering as a result. My endeavor is to continue this magnificent expression of life by giving back to those that made a difference.

Through an imaginary and magical evening of cuisine the seduction begins . . . and I welcome you to join me in this celebration.

THE BEGINNINGS

WHEN I WAS SEVEN years of age a life changing accident occurred that would affect me for the rest of my life. While playing with other children in a paddock, a neighbor who was shooting pigeons with a pellet rifle accidentally shot me in the left eye. It was so traumatic I ran all the way

home, crying my eyes out. My parents took me to St. Vincent's Hospital where the doctor examined me. It was so serious that the physician picked me up and told my parents that I had to remain in the hospital. As my mother and father were struggling to leave I let out a huge scream peeing all over myself and whom I thought was my abductor.

That accident had almost blinded my left eye. After lengthy tests the medical team were thinking of replacing it with a glass one. But my parents fought that decision.

So every week for six months I had to visit the hospital for exercises and tests. It really affected the way I saw things. So my lovely mother made sure that I always wore an amulet shaped like an eye to ward off evil. Ah, those Greeks, suspicions were a constant reminder life was not safe. Somehow the traumatic incident at that very young age created independence within me, and so I began to take charge of my life. I lost my innocence that terrible day when such negativity hit my youthful body with such force. That villain escaped town never to be seen again.

I started to travel on my own by bus to Maroubra beach in Sydney to explore those jagged cliffs where wild oysters, mussels and sea urchins thrived in abundance against the powerful sea. Equipped with a small knife, some lemons and bread I feasted on God's nature. Food as a seducer raised its beautiful head early in my life. Sometimes my family would gather together for

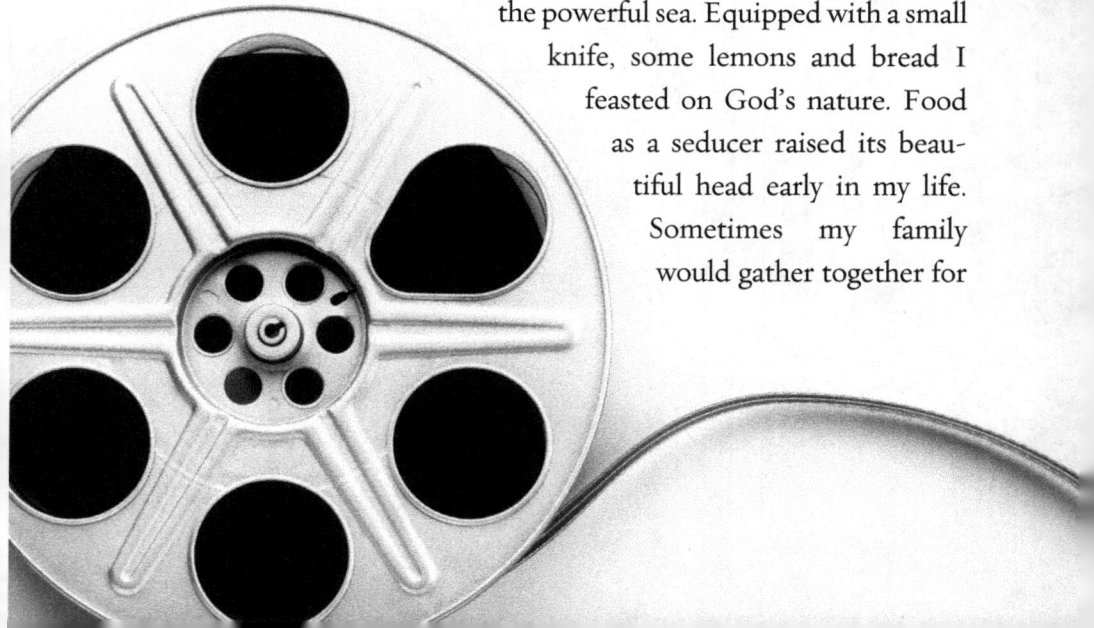

Octopi hanging over the rocks at Maroubra Beach, Sydney.

a picnic by the sea. I recall one Sunday afternoon while wading in the ocean, a large octopus wrapped itself around my leg. I let out a scream when my father, fully clothed, dived into the ocean and unhooked the struggling two-foot creature from my body. He grabbed it with his two hands while it was trying to escape and smashed it against the rocks, stunning the octopus. "Such bravado," I thought.

He did this ninety times until the tough, slippery cephalopod was tenderized and fit to eat. In those days they used to hang it on the clothesline for three weeks until it dried out and then it was grilled. An octopus has no blood—that's why it does not rot. Also the air in the 50's was not so polluted. It was a delicious appetizer and that barbequed aroma always made my mouth water.

Most of us who grew up with our "Families" had one thing in common: The food we tasted in our youth was while we were sitting at the dining table feasting on mother's cooking. That's when the education in nutrition began. Some of it we loved, some of it we got used to or simply never to repeat again. The Anglo-Australians were not comfortable in those days with foreign flavors brought to their land by European immigrants whose aromas filled the air. They were defensively calling us "A bunch of garlic munchers" or Wogs. But they soon got over all that when the next generation began to understand and love all these foreign flavors.

Imagine seeing a lamb's head floating in a big bowl of soup being served after the Greek Orthodox lent was over. And that was after midnight when you returned from the church ceremony already exhausted from guilt. It was not always a feast for the senses. I used to fall asleep at the table. But when you walked into the house there was always an aroma that told you what to expect. No matter what, it was a ceremony that begun with a prayer giving thanks for what we were about to receive. Father sat at the head of the table while mother always made sure her children ate every bite. We were not allowed to complain or talk unnecessarily while the ritual continued. What it taught us was respect: Respect for the food and culture, respect for our elders and the understanding of boundaries. Sadly these customs are so lost in today's world.

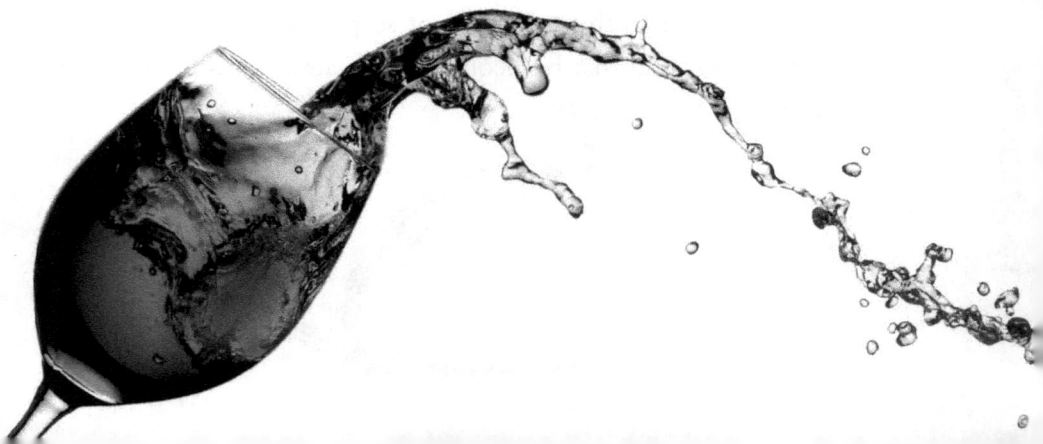

At eighteen, I had my first glass of wine and that made me feel like I was a grown-up because dad was sharing it with me, even though his glass always had more than mine. But who cares, it was a sign I was being accepted. Boy did that take a long time.

On early Saturday morning's Dad would take my brother George and myself to Paddy markets in Sydney, Australia to buy the weekly groceries. And our reward for carrying the heavy sacks back home while father strutted ahead empty handed? "A meat pie or a milk shake."

Kids, what we had to do for that favorite but elusive delicacy!

I would sometimes grow some carrots in our little back yard because I thought it would help mother through her struggles— even collecting beer and wine bottles from the alleys while the drunkards were passed out. I'd sell them to the bottle yard and make some money and fill mama's coffers with pennies. It's one of the reasons why she would say, "There goes my little gentleman with pennies in his pocket."

I suppose you would call it character building. But mother always appreciated when the gesture came from love and when things were tough her dinner plate always seemed to have less. You don't forget those sacrifices, those images, and those experiences that told you how well your parents were doing by what was served on the dinner table. And that is why I dreamed of America where abundance was apparent and the dream of becoming could be realized.

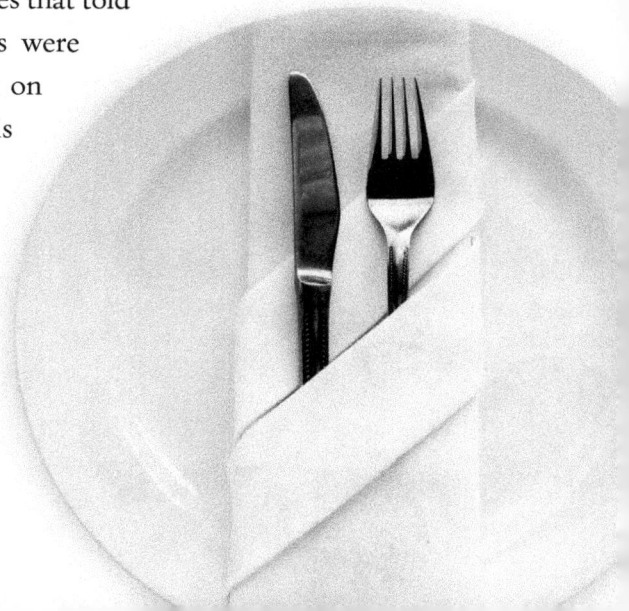

My dream did come true by going to America and with my wonderful success sent my parents to Europe many times. It helped them evolve as well, where the strains of the earlier years had become a memory. So now for the first time they were arriving in the United States with a stopover in Hawaii, to visit the son that got away on his own terms.

I arrived in Honolulu a day earlier to make sure their beginnings in America would be without conflict. But their plane from Sydney arrived earlier than expected and I discovered them waiting for me by their suitcases at Honolulu airport. They looked so vulnerable on their own, waiting for their eldest son to welcome them in a foreign land. It brought tears to my eyes. Our roles had switched and they were no longer the caretakers. I was finally the adult, and they were looking for my guidance. They beamed when they caught sight of me and we hugged each other passionately. They were here to experience a country that had embraced their son and now they felt safe at last.

After unpacking their belongings at the hotel they wanted to sit on the park bench and observe the multitude of foreigners parading along the boardwalk. Coming from Greece and Australia the sea was always part of their environment where the salt air was known to clear away their anxieties. I remembered what my spiritual teacher in California used to say, "When you are feeling too important, Thaao, why don't you go and stand in front of the ocean and see

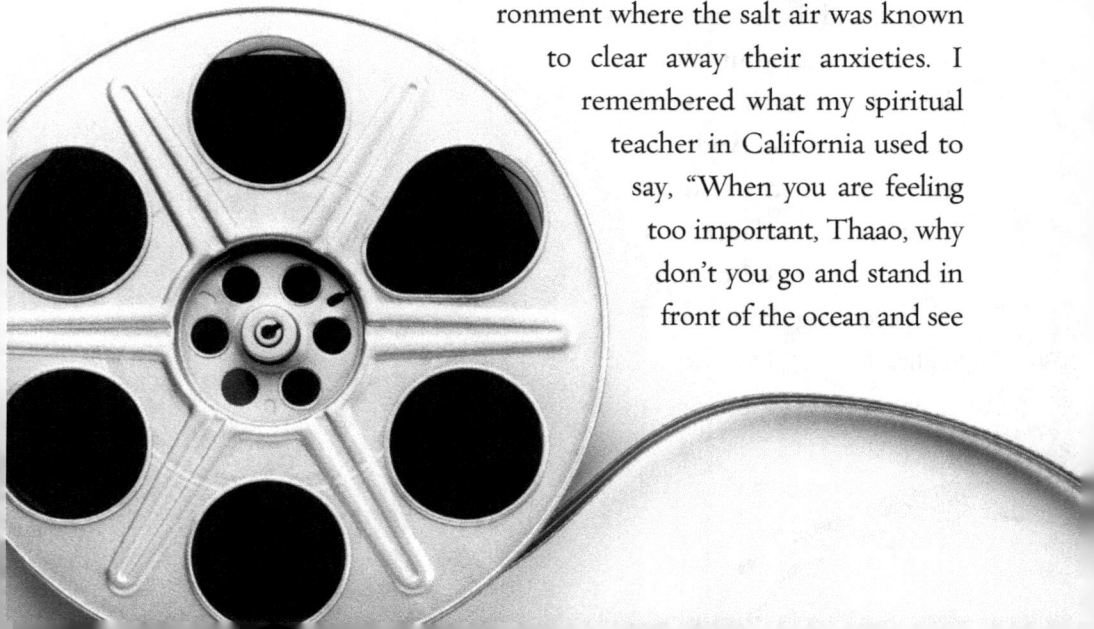

how small you are. It will teach you humility. That's good medicine for an actor."

Now it was time for my parents to experience the cuisine in Honolulu. They loved seafood as I did and so I took them to Michael's restaurant by the pier. It had a beautiful atmosphere, wonderfully operated with such courteous waiters; it put all of us at ease. My parents were impressed and now it was time to order. My mother kept smiling at me as if somewhere deep

Clams in black bean sauce.

down, her son that left so long ago brought some light to their existence.

"Where did you come from?" My mother asked. "You left us and came here all alone without a penny, America must be generous?"

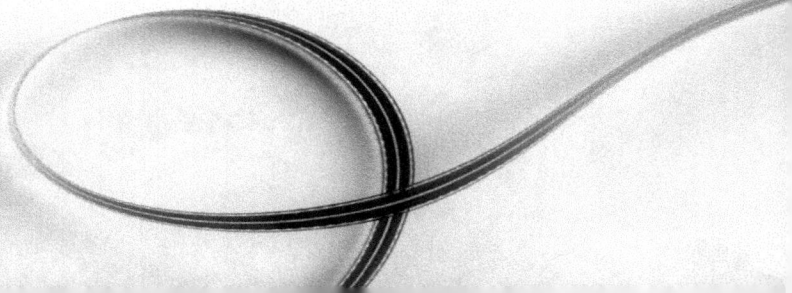

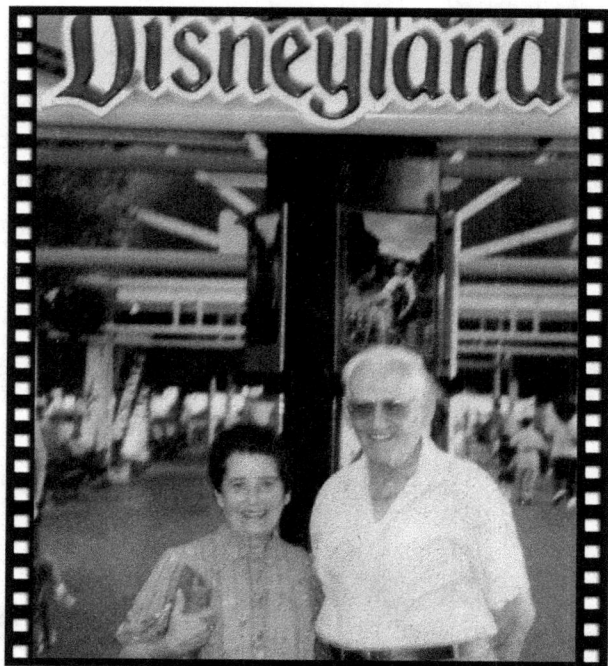

My father wanting the last word said proudly, "He took after me. Didn't I go to Australia from Greece at his age?"

"Ah yes, but look where he went. He's like his grandfather, who was a merchant," She responded proudly.

All three of us laughed together because nothing had really changed. They always played the game of whose family's heritage was the finest.

Mother was also happy that I was still wearing that little eye amulet that she gave me in my youth, always believing it would keep her son safe from negative forces. I told them that in my early years I remembered how my grandfather George would make his own olives and yogurt, how he would make organic preserved herring by putting bricks at the bottom of the tin can, adding lots of sea salt, then placing the fish over it. He continued the process until it reached the top, then poured water through the ingredients. After three months the fish was ready to eat, the olives marinated in his magic brew while the yogurt became thick and creamy in its protected space. I loved all that inventiveness from the culture I was brought up in. They were all so knowledgeable when it came to understanding the natural process in food making. It had a great influence on me especially when I was challenged to bring my own taste to the table when entertaining people in my industry.

My parents ordered their main courses but their biggest surprise was the enormity of its servings. My father looked at the size of his grilled whole snapper and thought it was for two. Feeling in heaven he responded,

"America is really generous, and why not? We are now its guests."

My mother had ordered her favorite dish, clams in a black bean sauce, hardly Greek. I had soft-shell crab with capers. I was in heaven, too.

They enjoyed their stay in America especially when they remained for six weeks at my home

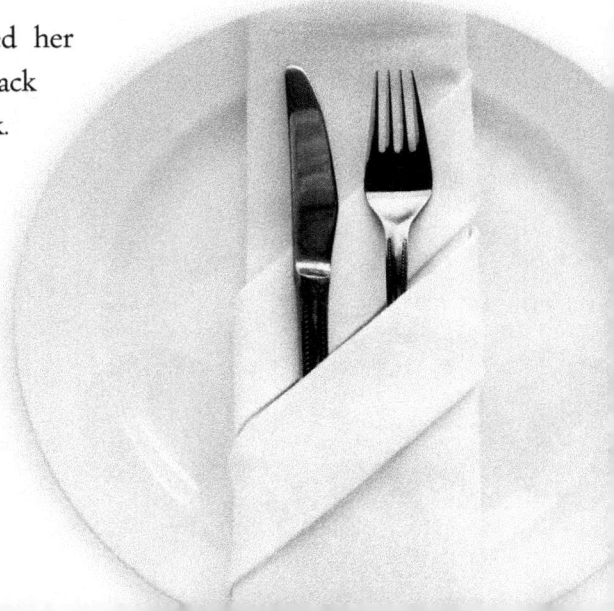

in Los Angeles high above the city in the Hollywood Hills. I took them to Disneyland, which they loved. They were children again and I realized how much I missed and loved them. Mother enjoyed being taken shopping, buying her favorite accessories, bags and shoes. She was proud of those experiences when for the first time in her life the young man she thought she had lost became the prodigal son that returned back on his terms and treated her like a queen. At last the struggles of her youth had disappeared and for mama it was like being in a movie where the fantasy of being able to say "I want that, that and that," was a reality. For my father a simple man, a few pair of shorts was all he needed. We would leave him at home while he enjoyed his card game of solitaire. He too needed time to reflect.

I cooked for them almost everyday trying to make up for the years I was absent from their world. My parents were surprised how a nice Greek boy from Australia had explored such diversity in cuisine.

I explained to them that the traditions of their heritage became the fabric that I continued to weave through my life in America, where I was able to explore the rituals of the past and make them my own in the present. And by doing that I continued to create a tapestry as a function for the next generation. That is the reason why I began to explore the idea of this book that came from a deep and personal place, that I wanted to

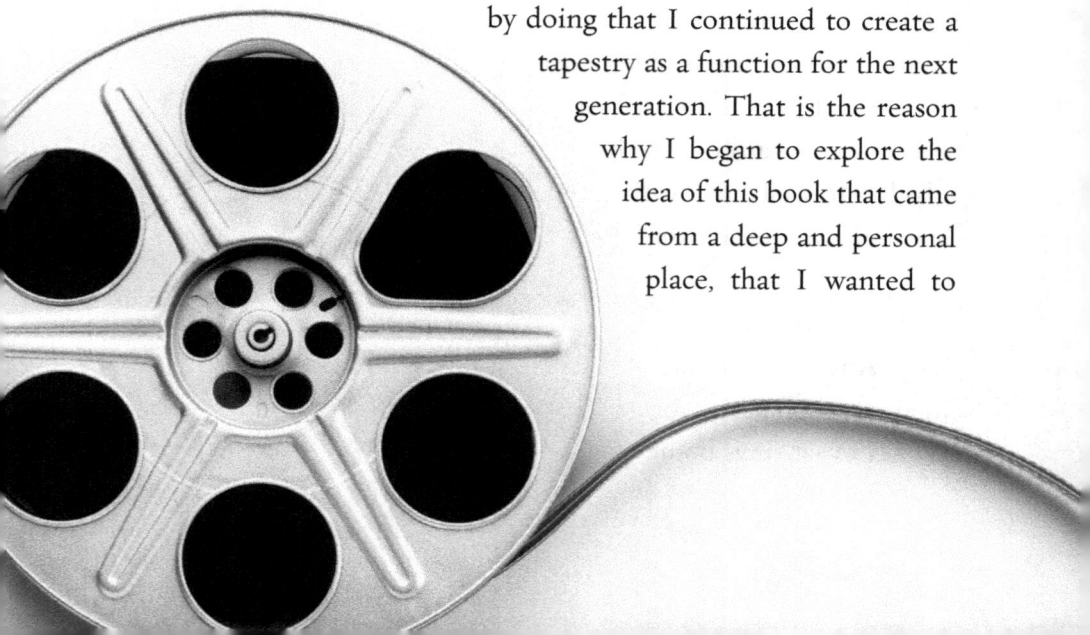

share those long-lived customs and traditions with the many lives that crossed my path.

When my parents were leaving I got permission to take them on board the plane to make sure they were comfortable. As I was saying good-bye the expression on their faces was enigmatic. They had at last shared the joys and success of a life they never had before. But for me, you see, I felt something unique: For the first time my parents were leaving me. All those years ago it was I who was always leaving them. Now, I understood their pain. We had come full circle and that for me was a revelation.

So in the spirit of my family, and the enormous rich culture they gifted me with, I share those riches with the guests that I am about to break bread with, real or imagined.

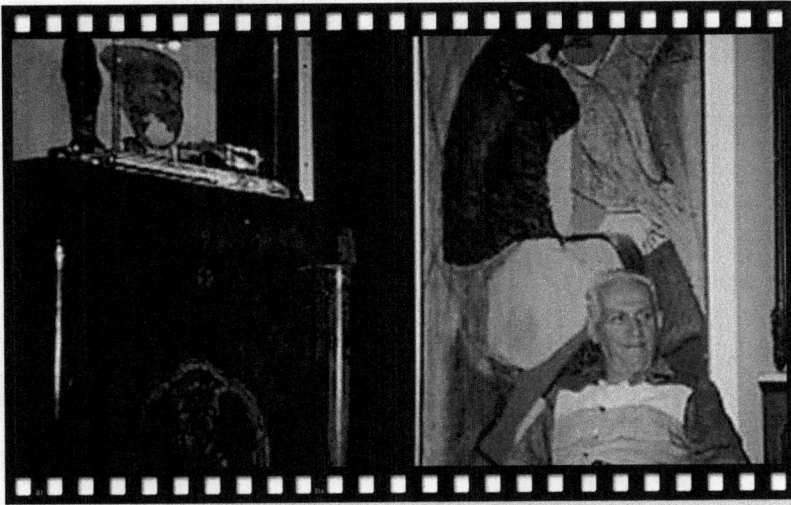

Dad relaxing at my home.

Me and Mum.

Me and Dad.

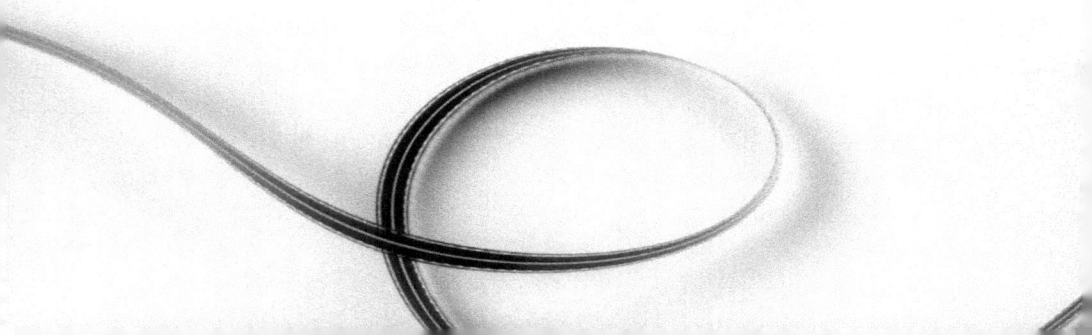

JACQUELINE KENNEDY

IN MY EARLY TWENTIES after living in New York for a year I
began working as an apprentice at
Ellsworth and Goldie, an art gallery
on East 52nd street in New York.
It housed the best collection
of South East Asian sculpture
in America. I was
surrounded by works of

exemplary beauty and enjoyed immersing my mind into the books and art in order to gain more knowledge. Our clients were rich private collectors and museum curators who would be admitted by appointment only. The fact that I could touch these ancient pieces, live with them daily, know their provenance was exhilarating for me. One afternoon while studying some of these rare pieces, there was a knock on the door. I reluctantly got up to answer it.

I opened the door to say "Sorry, appointments only" and was astonished to see American history standing before me: an elegant Jacqueline Kennedy was apologizing for showing up without an appointment. I was elated, but kept my composure. She told her two bodyguards to remain outside while she explored the gallery. I asked her if she would like some tea and surprisingly she graciously accepted.

I quickly called upstairs to Massahiro, the Japanese houseman, and instructed him to make tea for our special guest.

He laughed and scoffed. "You joking. Apprentice like you not order such a thing, and with Ellsworth's best silver? You crazy?"

As Mrs. Kennedy walked past the elevator, the door suddenly opened, revealing Massahiro standing in shorts. When he saw her he gasped "Oh my God," placed his hands over his mouth and repeatedly bowed in apology. The doors closed as I escorted our distinguished guest to the back of the gallery to a room three stories high

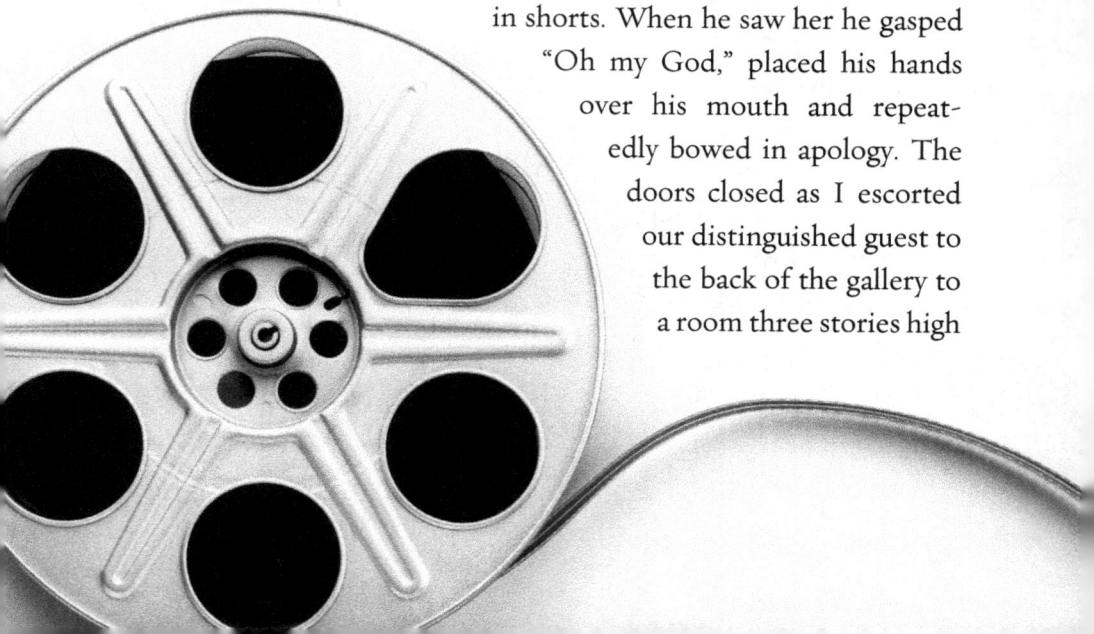

filled with the best private collection of South East Asian sculpture in the world.

The ceiling was made of glass and was designed to reflect the changing light of the New York skyline. It was still grey outside, making the large studio seem like a tomb. It was all meticulously lit by Ellsworth, who had a brilliant eye. Every piece told a story. Arrogant as he was, the man had phenomenal taste and was a greatly respected expert in his field.

Mrs. Kennedy sat in her element, asking me to tell her the origin of the ancient pieces. Massahiro brought a tray filled with shortbread and tea. He must have raided the safe. Dressed in his proper costume along with his cool Oriental manner he poured the tea. As he was leaving he looked my way with scorn and envy as if to say, "You lucky bastard."

I spent an hour with Jacqueline Kennedy. The knowledge I accumulated under Ellsworth's direction was priceless. I told her that the Chinese always believed that the spirit of the artist was with their creation forever. That was something I picked up from him during the seduction of a potential buyer. They were rare pieces from Vietnam, China, India and Japan dating from the 2nd century B.C. Han period to the Ming Dynasty in 16th century A.D.

As I joined her for tea, she inquired about my Greek heritage. I expounded upon the subject and spoke passionately about the culture from which I escaped. She appeared to be really interested, an eager student of life.

She was beautifully dressed with that famous pillbox hat and possessed a truly sophisticated manner. It was easy to see why she had been a First Lady and was so greatly admired by her

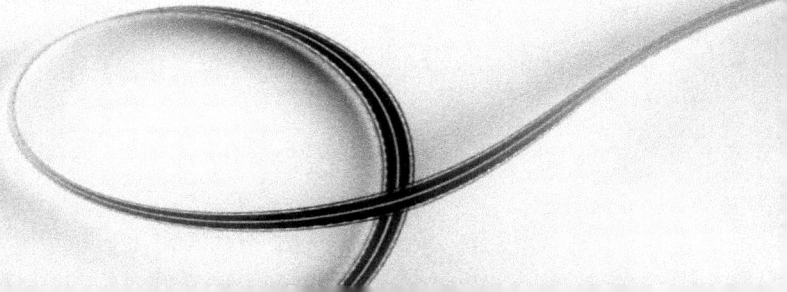

country. Our exchange took place in only one hour, but the timing was extraordinary and it furthered my belief that I hadn't made a mistake coming to New York. For the first time, I had a sense of success because I no longer felt like that Greek immigrant from Australia looking for the right path.

When Robert Ellsworth returned from lunch, he asked me if anyone important had called or come in.

"Yes, Jacqueline Kennedy," I said, beaming.

He kept walking up the stairs, mocking me. "Sure, sure, sure."

Meanwhile, a call came in from Jacqueline Kennedy, interested in a head sculpture from China that I had shown her. To Ellsworth's surprise—and dismay—she was only interested in speaking with me. He bantered on about who he was and how he was more equipped to handle the transaction. The former First Lady insisted on talking to the apprentice—and only the apprentice. His ego badly bruised, Ellsworth handed me the phone with contempt. I had my first sale.

Three weeks later Jacqueline Kennedy married Aristotle Onassis. The joke among my family and friends was she had to meet up with another Greek to make up her mind.

I imagined if I had invited Jackie Kennedy-Onassis for dinner, what cuisine would be on the menu? Greek, of course.

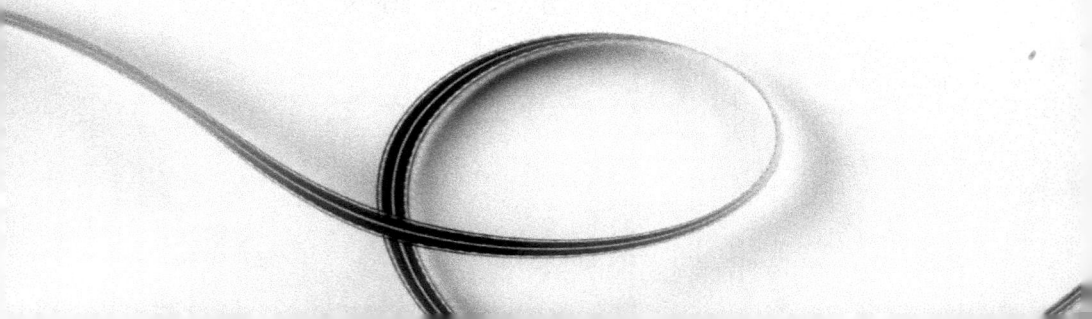

INGREDIENTS

1 whole organic chicken

1 bay leaf

3 lemons

1 cup white rice

2 eggs

2 cloves of garlic

2 slices of butter

salt and pepper to taste

chopped parsley

INSTRUCTIONS

Boil the whole chicken in a large pot of water for an hour with the bay leaf. Drain chicken and set aside. Squeeze the juice of the two lemons into the broth and add two garlic cloves with two slices of butter. Salt and pepper to taste. Pour the rice into the broth until done. (30 Mins)

In a separate bowl beat the whites of two eggs until stiff. Add the egg yolks and beat. Take two cups of the broth and stir into the egg mixture.

Slowly add to the broth and stir. Add more lemons if you want to enhance the flavor. Serve into bowls with strips of chicken and chopped parsley. Serves 4.

INGREDIENTS

6 medium size eggplants

3 pounds ground beef

1 large onion

salt and pepper

4 tablespoons Herb de Provence

2 large garlic clove, finely minced

1 pound canned sliced tomatoes

¾ quarters cup tomato puree

1 pound sliced mushrooms

6 tablespoons flour

white pepper

4 cups hot milk

6 eggs

3 cups grated Parmesan cheese

3 cinnamon sticks

INSTRUCTIONS

Peel all the eggplants as I found the skin could be bitter. Slice thinly and pan fry lightly in olive oil. Set aside in a colander to drain the oil and cover. In a large pan brown the mincemeat in olive oil. When done, cover the meat so it does not dry. Take the chopped onion and garlic and lightly brown adding salt, pepper, pepper and salt. Stir and add the chopped mushrooms until done. Mix in the sliced tomatoes and the tomato purée. Cook together for ten minutes and finally add the mincemeat and sticks of cinnamon. Cover and slowly cook for an hour, stirring every fifteen minutes.

In a large baking pan place a layer of eggplant until the base is covered. Cover entire pan with the meat mixture and pour Parmesan cheese across the top. Repeat the process three times until the layer reaches almost the top of the pan.

The Béchamel sauce begins with melting a stick of butter and at the same time heat the milk so it will be ready with the final stage of the sauce. Add salt and pepper along with the flour stirring constantly so the paste doesn't stick. Slowly pour the hot milk into the mixture and keep stirring so it won't curdle. Beat up the eggs and add one cup of the sauce into the eggs and mix it together thoroughly. Add the egg mixture into the sauce stirring quickly and then turn off the heat.

Add the Béchamel sauce over the top of the pan, covering the entire layer, and generously sprinkle over the Parmesan cheese.

Bake the Moussaka for an hour. When the top is golden brown remove and let stand for a minimum twenty minutes.

Sprinkle finely chopped parsley over the dish, cut in squares and serve. I sometimes will place the Moussaka over a helping of mashed potatoes with a Greek salad comprised of Arugula, sliced watermelon, thin slices of red onion and chopped goat's cheese. Serves 4.

INGREDIENTS

2 sticks unsalted butter (soft)

6 tablespoons cane sugar

1 egg yolk

tablespoon Brandy

2 ¼ cups flour

whole cloves

INSTRUCTIONS

Beat butter and sugar until creamy. Add yolk and brandy beating thoroughly. Slowly beat in the sifted flour and mix thoroughly. With hands, form small squares and place a whole clove in its center. Place the Kourambiedes on a sheet in a pre-heated (350° F.) and cook for 35 minutes. When done let the biscuits cool off completely before covering them with cane sugar. Serve with Greek coffee. Serves 4.

It was a rare privilege to spend time with this great lady who did not disappoint. Her curiosity with life and its beauty, her grace inspired me in my youth to continue to explore and appreciate the best of what crossed my path. Jacqueline Kennedy was indeed something to celebrate.

OMAR SHARIF

OMAR SHARIF WAS ONE of my favorite actors ever since I first saw him in the classic *Lawrence of Arabia*. When Director Gary Nelson asked me to work with him again in the mini-series *Memories of Midnight* with Jane Seymour, I did not hesitate. Shot mainly in Yugoslavia and Greece, the story was loosely based on the rivalry of Greek shipping magnates Onassis and Niarchos.

On the first day in the make-up trailer in Zagreb, Omar sat next to me. When introduced, he simply responded with a nod. Appearing on the set, which was the actual house of ex-President Tito, Sharif made his majestic entrance and announced to me, "When I knock you down and you go flying over this 18th century table please don't break it."

"Oh Mr. Sharif, if I let you knock me down in our first scene together we will have nowhere to go for the rest of the story. After all I am your nemesis," I responded.

Suddenly the ice was broken and he embraced me with open arms, shouting out to the director, "I love this actor!"

Now he looked upon me as a trusted thespian and whispered, "Do you like Champagne and caviar?"

Surprised by his sudden shift in behavior I quickly replied "Of course."

"Good, after we break for lunch, come to my trailer and we will celebrate."

During lunch, he told me that I reminded him of his only son but "the idiot could have married better." I asked him about *Lawrence of Arabia*, and he loved telling me the tales that Peter O'Toole and he had experienced in Aqaba, Jordan. Because of the lengthy shoot and boredom and desert heat, they would drink so much they had to be tied to the camels so they wouldn't fall off. He talked about the many languages he spoke, five in all that allowed him to play so many colorful and diverse roles. I was surprised when he mentioned he was born a Catholic in Alexandria but converted to Islam after his marriage to his Egyptian wife.

We spoke also of his greatest film *Doctor Zhivago*. He laughed like a little boy when he shared with me David Lean's tough direction on the first day's shoot: "I want to see the poetry of the film through

your eyes, I want you to do nothing, not to emote, not to have a reaction, just be." I instantly recalled those steady eyes as *Zhivago* that made that face and performance a classic.

When Omar had to go back to Paris and finish shooting another film, he came back exhausted. He couldn't remember his lines and he kept flubbing. The director, knowing that Omar and I had developed a close relationship, took a break and asked me to take our star behind the curtain and have a talk. I did and in private. Omar had a breakdown and cried on my shoulder. I will never forget that moment when he trusted me with his emotions. Vulnerable as he was we went back and shot the scene with his professionalism intact. He never faulted. He was a man who had worked with many great stars and made so many classic films that his expectations were high.

When I said goodbye to Omar, a great sadness washed over me. He left me with such poignant memories especially of the man that lived well. When I look back at those times his influences had become part of me; they sharpened my being and sense of perspective of living in the now without regrets. We were all capable of being royalty.

On July 10, 2015, the Egyptian matinee idol that enthralled the audiences worldwide died of a heart attack at a Cairo hospital. He was 83. In his last years Alzheimer's had began to take its toll, something he was afraid of when we had worked together. He invited me to visit him and show me Paris. I never did take him up on his offer and that I regret, especially now.

If a dinner at my house had become a reality this is what I would have presented to this wonderful star that was Omar.

INGREDIENTS

2 tablespoons unsalted butter

1 large onion, diced

3 celery ribs, diced

2 large carrots, diced

4 garlic cloves, minced

1 teaspoon ground cumin

½ teaspoon ground coriander

½ teaspoon chili powder

½ teaspoon hot curry powder

2 quarts chicken or vegetable stock

One 14.5 ounce can diced tomatoes

2 cups red lentils

salt and pepper to taste

INSTRUCTIONS

In a large stockpot melt the butter over medium heat. Add the onions, celery, carrots, and garlic and sauté until soft, about 10-15 minutes. Add the cumin, coriander, chili powder, and curry powder and stir to coat the veggies with the spices. Cook over medium heat for a few minutes to toast the spices. Add the tomatoes and the stock and bring to a simmer. Season generously with salt and pepper and add the lentils. Simmer for about 30-40 minutes, until lentils and vegetables are very soft.

In a few batches, purée the soup in a food processor until completely smooth. Transfer back to pot and season with salt and pepper to taste. If you like it a bit spicier, you can add a little cayenne pepper and more black pepper. I've always liked extra cumin and curry.

Serve with flatbread wedges and top with a bit of Greek yogurt mixed with lemon juice. I also garnished the soup with some roasted chickpeas and fresh chives. There are millions of recipes out there for roasted chickpeas, but basically just rinse and dry off some canned chickpeas (or my preferred name, garbanzo beans), toss them with a bit of olive oil and whatever seasonings you like, and roast them on a baking sheet in a really hot oven (400 F) until they are crispy. I just added all of the spices that I used in the soup along with some chopped garlic and they are a perfect compliment to the creamy soup and tangy yogurt. Serves 4.

INGREDIENTS

6 tablespoons extra-virgin olive oil

6 lamb shanks, trimmed and Frenched

sea salt and freshly ground black pepper

4 cups chicken stock

8 cloves garlic, crushed

¾ cup maple syrup

½ cup brown sugar

½ cup malt vinegar

peel of one orange

½ cup orange juice

4 rosemary sprigs

½ cup pomegranate seeds

MINT SAUCE

¾ cup malt vinegar

1 cup brown sugar

2 cups mint leaves, finely chopped

INSTRUCTIONS

Preheat oven to 350° F. Heat oil in large frying pan. Sprinkle salt and pepper on the shanks and brown on all sides. Place in a deep-sided roasting pan and set aside.

In a saucepan, add the stock, garlic, maple syrup, peel, juice and rosemary. Bring to a boil and pour over the shanks. Cover with foil and roast the shanks for 2 1/2 hours, turning once.

Increase oven temp to 425° F.

Remove the foil and roast the shanks, turning every 15 minutes for another 45 to 50 minutes or until they are sticky and glossy.

While the shanks are cooking, make the mint sauce.

Place the vinegar and sugar in a saucepan and stir until combined. Bring to a boil and cook for 5-6 minutes or until thickened. Remove from heat allow to cool. Add the fresh mint, stirring for a couple of minutes. Place the lamb shanks on a serving plate. Serve lamb with pan juices and mint sauce. Sprinkle pomegranate over individual dishes. Serves 4.

INGREDIENTS

2 sticks butter

¾ cup sugar

1 egg

½ cup semolina

1 cup orange juice

3 cups self-raising flour

1 tablespoon cinnamon

1 teaspoon orange rind, grated

honey

crushed walnuts, sugar and cinnamon

INSTRUCTIONS

Cream butter and sugar. Beat in egg.

Sift in flour, semolina, cinnamon and orange rind, alternately with orange juice.

Mix well.

Shape individually into fingers and lightly press with fork.

Bake in oven at 350° F. until golden brown for 30 minutes.

Switch off oven and leave to cool.

Heat honey and dip biscuits.

Roll in combination of walnuts, sugar and cinnamon. Serves 4.

I would serve them with Champagne, as Mr. Sharif always loved sharing that with me. He loved engaging in the pleasures of life and celebrating the similarities of new unions.

GEORGE CLOONEY

In the 1980's I used to work out at the YMCA in HOL-LYWOOD where many young actors came together in this friendly watering hole. No matter what success you had acquired everyone behaved normally because of this down to earth atmosphere. Whether it was in the weight room or the basketball court everyone got to know each other. George Clooney went often before he became an international movie star. He loved his basketball game and on occasion I joined the group or observed his team from the weight room. Always friendly and that face that smiled upon anyone who was in his presence, it

was no surprise how extraordinary the acclaim in all facets of show business was conquered by this most loved human.

I remember a conversation about his wonderful father. Nick Clooney made sure his family which was very close-knit, and was always home in the evenings for dinner, often discussing current events. I think George's early conditioning made him the Renaissance man he is today. Also, George and his father helped to bring the "Darfur Genocide," the mass slaughter and rape in Western Sudan, to the world's consciousness.

Having been recently married to British-Lebanese barrister Amal Alamuddin in a private ceremony in Venice, Italy, my thought immediately went to the idea that the only thing Clooney has to conquer is in the political arena. So before he becomes even more famous I imagined what wonderful cuisine I would serve this amazing couple. Living in Lake Cuomo Italy I decided that my first course would be?

Served over a red slice of an heirloom tomato, and above the crab cake a medium poached egg, topped with hollandaise sauce and a generous serving of caviar.

INGREDIENTS

1 pound fresh lump crab

1 egg

1 tablespoon Worcestershire sauce

1 pack Old Bay Crab Cake Mix

6 tablespoons mayonnaise

1 finely chopped red onion

1 finely chopped garlic clove

pepper

5 tablespoons Japanese bread-crumbs

1 sliced red heirloom tomato

4 poached eggs (medium)

olive oil or butter

caviar

Japanese seaweed

INSTRUCTIONS

Mix into the crabmeat egg, Worcestershire sauce, crab mix, onion and garlic, pepper, breadcrumbs and mayonnaise. Form patties and roll in Japanese breadcrumbs.

Pan fry the crab patties until golden brown. On top of the sliced heirloom tomato place a crab cake and spread a little mayonnaise on top. Then place the poached egg on top with Hollandaise sauce and add the final touch, a teaspoon of caviar surrounded by a salad. Sprinkle seaweed around the crab and serve. Serves 4.

INGREDIENTS

1 whole Branzino fish, cleaned

olive oil

lemons

oregano

salt and pepper

melted butter

INSTRUCTIONS

Baste Branzino fish with olive oil, lemon juice and oregano, salt and pepper. Turn on the broiler high and in a deep pan pour a ½ inch of water. Place fish on rack and broil for 10 minutes each side basting it every 5 minutes with olive oil and lemon juice. When done place fish on a plate and top it with lemon butter, chopped parsley and then serve. Serves 4.

Serve with lemon grilled asparagus.

INGREDIENTS

8 eggs

10 tablespoons semolina

8 tablespoons blanched almonds, chopped

8 tablespoons sugar

1 cup orange juice

! tablespoon grated orange rind

¼ cup ouzo

1 teaspoon vanilla

SYRUP

2 cups sugar

1 cup water

6 drops lemon juice

½ cup crushed walnuts

INSTRUCTIONS

First make the syrup. Boil all ingredients together and simmer for ten minutes and set aside.

Beat egg yolks with sugar till fluffy. Add vanilla, ouzo and orange rind and continue beating. Add semolina, almonds and orange juice. Beat the egg whites till stiff and fold into mixture lightly. Pour into greased baking dish.

Bake in oven at 375° F. for 35 minutes. Remove from oven and set aside. Pour the warm syrup until the cake absorbs the liquid. Decorate with finely chopped walnuts or almonds. When chilled, cut the semolina cake into diamond or square shapes and serve with Vanilla ice cream. Serves 4.

George Clooney crossed my path briefly. His personal stamp on everything that he did from acting, movie making, important world causes made a difference with all of us. His image is one of the best examples of what Hollywood created. He got his breaks and made them his own, ever tasteful, ever the consummate professional with class. And in my mind brought joy to the imagined world I shared with him and his wife Amal.

BARBRA STREISAND
AND SHIRLEY MACLAINE

ONE AFTERNOON I DROPPED by a brunch in the Hollywood Hills where Barbra Streisand, Shirley Maclaine, Bella Abzug and the wonderful artist Ann Farrell were sitting around a table discussing an affair one of them was having with Prime Minister Pierre Trudeau of Canada. Standing in the kitchen, my ears had popped up when his assets and passion became the subject of discussion. One of them said, "When you're finished with him, can I call him?" As only a star with audacity could ask. I'd heard enough and since no one was aware of my presence, I made some noise to alert them I was there. The conversation

stopped abruptly and Annie came out to see who was in her kitchen. We were old friends and I had just dropped by to deliver a Greek dessert as a favor. "I'd ask you in, Thaao, but the conversation is very personal." "No kidding" I replied. As I was leaving I heard them ask, "Who was that?" "My Greek Lover," she said. Someone said, "bring him back," as I walked out the door without looking back.

Three days later I was asked to have a read-through of the mini-series *Out on a Limb* based on Shirley Maclaine's novel. At the roundtable were Maclaine and the actor Tom Hulce, producers and the writers. I was reading the part of her lover, a politician from Australia. Charles Dance would eventually play the role in the television production. It was a true story that enveloped Shirley's spiritual saga in Machu Picchu, Peru.

Shirley had great energy and a powerful and determined gait. Everyone was introduced and Shirley quickly sat in front of me, eyes direct, legs apart and said, "Start." I was more amused than intimidated by the behavior. But I loved how fear somehow didn't reside in her mind. I was facing a champion and she demanded that in return. Back and forward the dialogue went. Hulce was terrific as her adventurous guide and I played the love aspect as convincing as possible. Half way through she asked re the politician. "Thaao brought a sensitivity to the part that was not in the script and I like it a lot. Can we keep that in?" With that she came up to me and gave me a great embrace.

"Thanks for bringing that to the table," she said. And with that she smiled for the first time.

We continued through the rest of the day with great success. At the end of it Shirley mentioned a four-day seminar she was holding in Los Angeles and invited me to attend. It was through this totally new experience that metaphysics again returned to my playground, with new voices waiting to be heard. In a hotel near LAX, four hundred people gathered together and meditated as the host elevated our spirit through music and words that helped sing out the potential and eventual recognition of self.

Shirley told us great stories of how she went through her own adventures, overcoming the obstacles and managing and moving through each experience. That kept sharpening the tools she brought in, while enhancing her work as an actor by being in the present. I thought it a great event and an addition to the life experiences I would carry with me. Meditation for me became the source I would go to for healing, understanding and for those questions I could not answer. Shirley was a sign-post that told me I was on the right path.

Streisand and I met at a luncheon in the Hollywood Hills in the 90's when she was involved with Jon Peters of Columbia Studios. He used to be a famous hairdresser and eventually became a successful producer. We were intro-duced by a close friend who had obviously dis-cussed my passion for cooking. Very attractive but smaller in height, I expected this giant

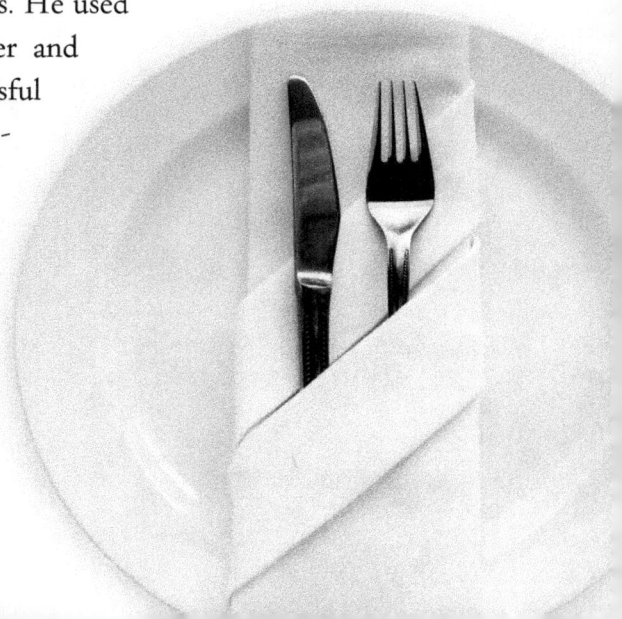

of our industry to be taller with that amazing voice. Her first response was "I hear you're a great cook?" I responded nervously, "Well I like to eat well." The conversation continued for a few more minutes about what I liked to eat and she shared her favorite recipes. Down to earth and not disappointing she recalled her love of all foods including Greek and French cuisine. I loved the way she naturally flirted which allowed her sensuality to embrace the person she was talking to. For a brief moment she made me feel that what I shared was intimate and knowing. Warm and shy she allowed me in. Before our conversation had ended Jon Peters interrupted and abruptly took her away. "That was brusque," I thought. Well at least I had a moment with that *Funny Lady* that wasn't exactly lunch, but it was memorable.

So if I did invite Shirley and Barbara to lunch I imagined these great minds sharing their world of politics and the pleasure they would receive from the seduction of food. This would have been my celebration to them.

So while the sun is shining let's stir the appetite for these two international icons.

INGREDIENTS

1½ tablespoons peanut oil

2 tablespoons finely chopped fresh ginger

2 teaspoons chopped garlic

3 tablespoons finely chopped scallions

1½ raw shrimp shelled and deveined

SAUCE

4 tablespoons sweet chile sauce

2 tablespoons apple cider vinegar

1 teaspoon salt

I teaspoon pepper

1 tablespoon sesame oil

2 teaspoon sugar

chopped cilantro to garnish

INSTRUCTIONS

Heat a pan over high heat. Add the oil, when hot add the ginger, garlic, and scallions. Fry for 25 seconds, then add the shrimp, and fry for another 1 minute. Add the sauce ingredients and continue. Toss for another 3 minutes over high heat.

Serve at once with chopped cilantro. Serves 3.

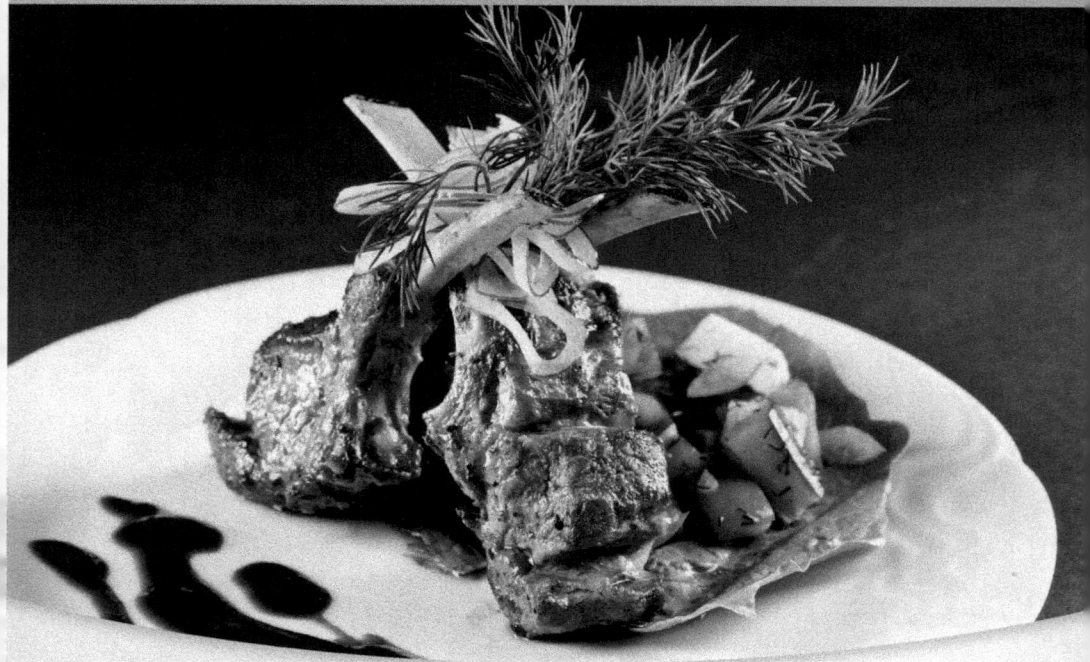

INGREDIENTS

2 racks of lamb (8 ribs each)

4 tablespoons sweet honey soy sauce

2 tablespoons fresh rosemary

2 minced garlic cloves

red onion

salt and pepper

INSTRUCTIONS

Let the marinated lamb in honey soy sauce sit out of refrigerator 1½ hours before cooking, sprinkled with chopped rosemary and crushed garlic cloves. Add salt and pepper. Before putting into broiler oven wrap bone ends with foil.

Turn on broiler and in a deep pan fill with one inch of water. Place the lamb face down onto a rack and broil both sides for about 15 minutes each side until crispy brown.

Note: I always use water when broiling lamb, poultry or fish as it keeps the meat moist on the inside whereas the broiler makes it crisp on the outside.

When ready to serve I baste the lamb with the soy sauce and rosemary, as it gives the lamb a wonderful exotic taste.

Garnish with sprig of rosemary and shaved red onion. Serves 3.

Sorbet is always a wonderful and simple way to cleanse the palette.

Some actors I've worked with always had their egos present and their hearts frozen and because of those bad memories, I had a hard time watching their work
later, let alone the thought of sharing a feast. But these two iconic, multi-faceted
women, Streisand and Maclaine, one I had dinner with, the other, well almost, allowed me in for that short time, and shared with me, a life.

"Memories light the corners of my mind."

JOAN RIVERS

IN THE MID SEVENTIES Warren Burton, a friend from my acting class in Beverly Hills asked me to share a ride with him to Vegas. Joan Rivers had asked the favor of escorting her daughter Melissa Rivers to Nevada. Warren used to introduce Joan in a small club in Los Angeles when she wanted to test out her new material before she would perform to a larger audience in Vegas. I went to see her a few times and found her hysterical. Her early material wasn't as mean as it was in her later years. Her mean antics about Stars who paraded on the red carpet during Oscar season were legendary. But as a female comedian Joan pioneered for others to follow in her footsteps. She became the

mother of them all. Shocking at times but self-deprecating she managed to survive well in a male dominant arena. I loved her most of the time when her brilliance shone beyond the obvious put down.

Melissa then aged six, was escorted by car from Los Angeles to Las Vegas where her mother was performing at Caesars. She was a lovely little girl, well behaved and all the way through the desert we sang songs to entertain and keep her occupied. She missed her mother dearly.

Melissa had fallen asleep in my arms after the long five-hour drive. We arrived at Caesars where Joan was staying and as soon as she saw her baby she emotionally cried," Oh my baby, my baby." She was a great mother and lovely to see that behind the acerbic wit was a human being who openly showed her emotions. Now she was ready to go on with her show, now that her base was secure.

Joan Rivers was extraordinary that night, her sharp wit and the lethal delivery kept people in stitches. She was rather cruel about Elizabeth Taylor and her weight, her husbands, that was a bit off-putting, but otherwise that brilliant mind that shone belonged to a killer, a female that survived Hollywood land.

The next morning she invited us to breakfast. So simple, no star, just a lovely human being who was forever curious about life and new associates. She was charming and warm when she spoke of others as I was wondering when the biting humor

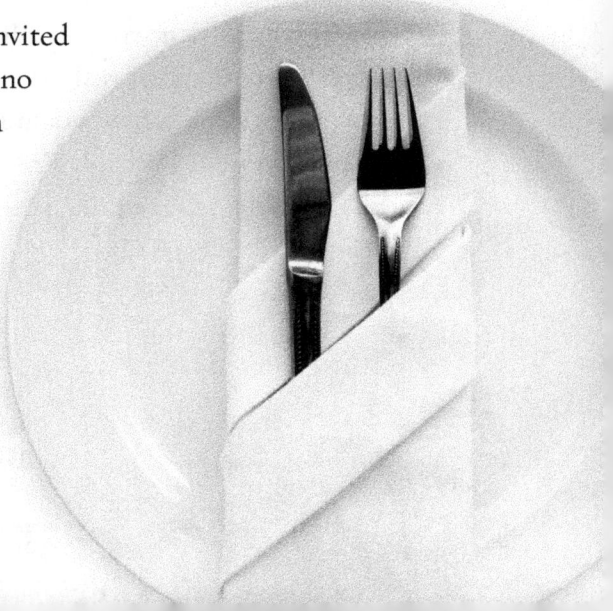

would come out. But that I discovered belonged on the stage and now she was with people she seemed to trust and not the pressure of having to perform. She invited us back again that night to see her show and dinner afterwards.

That afternoon I felt really sick from something I ate and had no choice but to stay in bed. Warren explained my absence and Joan was sorry to hear that. About 9 p.m. that night I was feeling better and not having been to Vegas before decided to walk around the hotel. I landed at a roulette table watching gambling enthusiasts groan when losses were taking place. Occasionally a winner would shout with joy keeping people's hopes up that their moment was about to arrive. Out of nowhere I heard a cynical voice say in passing, "Well obviously you recovered quickly?" Embarrassed I turned to see it was Joan Rivers, who continued laughing her head off. "It's okay darling you've already seen the show." I wanted to explain but the star was off to entertain her next audience. I never saw her again until ten years later when she was doing a cameo in a film I was starring in with Dame Edna, *Les Patterson Saves the World*. She over-played the American President with her wonderful comedic ability, and that was Joan. But, alas, I never saw her uniqueness again in person and in September 2014 she tragically past away.

So in remembrance of Joan Rivers who had, apart from her dangerous mouth, possessed great taste in jewelry, clothes and the finer things in life, how would I have celebrated her life with the cuisine chosen? Probably French, because her apartment in New York was designed like you would have walked into the Palace of Versailles.

INGREDIENTS

16 large scallops

1 stick of butter

4 tablespoon capers, drained

fresh lemon juice

1 tespoon white pepper

4 tablespoons chopped parsley

plain flour

INSTRUCTIONS

Coat scallops with flour. In a medium sized skillet melt 2 tablespoons butter over medium-high. Add scallops until golden brown (3 minutes). Transfer to plate and add the remaining butter to the liquid until brown.

Quickly add the capers, stir and pour over scallops with finely chopped parsley and serve immediately. Serves 6.

Served in a French White Clam Sauce

INGREDIENTS

1 pound fresh linguine

2 dozen medium sized clams

1 stick of butter

1 large onion

3 garlic cloves

1 teaspoon white pepper

2 tablespoons finely chopped parsley

1/2 cup bread crumbs

4 tablespoons sour cream

1 tablespoon red pepper flakes

INSTRUCTIONS

In a large pan, melt half the stick of butter adding white pepper, finely chopped onion and garlic until onion is translucent. Rinse clams and boil in 3 glasses of water until clams have opened. Set aside.

Pour the juice into the sautéed onions and stir. Add the remaining butter and parsley. When butter has melted add the breadcrumbs stirring in the sour cream for 2 minutes. Then add the clams without the shells. Cover until the linguine in cooked. Drain the pasta. Add desired red pepper flakes to the sauce.

Mix together and serve at once with toasted French bread. Garnish with clams in the shell. Serves 6.

Note: This is a great sauce to use for baked clams.

INGREDIENTS

6 ripe Bartlett pears

1 cup sugar

6 ounces of butter

1 cinnamon Stick

¾ cup heavy cream

vanilla ice cream

INSTRUCTIONS

Preheat oven to 350° F. Slice pears into quarters. Place the pears in a baking dish adding the thinly sliced butter, sugar and cinnamon stick over the pears. Bake for 45 minutes, basting the pears every 15 minutes until the fruit is tender and the sugar begins to crystalize. Remove the pears, discarding cinnamon stick and add the heavy cream to the crystallized sauce. Blend it in until it caramelizes and pour hot over the pears.

Serve at once with a scoop of vanilla ice cream. Serves 6.

Joan Rivers died the summer of 2014. Before her untimely and tragic death she was still glamorous and feisty as ever and at the top of her game. Joan always kept inventing herself, fighting those who always tried to limit her by pushing the envelope and shocking those who dared to question her method of comedy. She certainly had her share of tragedy when her lovely and gracious husband Edgar Rosenberg who I had met earlier, committed suicide. She was quoted as saying of her relationship, "It was a good match. We filled each other's gaps like two pieces of a puzzle. I gave him warmth. He gave me style."

And that she had in spades. This icon that crossed my path twice taught me resilience and that humor elevates the spirit and sometimes at a price. She will be missed by many but I'm sure she is somewhere special testing out her method of humor, beginning with "Can we talk?" - and making God laugh too.

BARRY HUMPHRIES /
DAME EDNA

From the film set of *Les Patterson Saves the World.*

ONE OF THE GREATEST and most memorable experiences I've had in the industry was with "Dame Edna," whom I consider to be one of the most hilarious human beings of the 20th century. His real name was Barry Humphries, but with costume, a wig and a high-pitched voice he morphs into a suburban housewife and international celebrity. A great star in England and an Australian treasure, his wicked humor consistently has people laughing in the aisles.

I met Barry in the late 80's in a restaurant in Sydney. He made a great entrance with a black cape and hat and then

proceeded to check me out. They were looking for an Australian actor to play Dame Edna's love interest in *Les Patterson Saves the World* directed by George Miller. I passed the test and we hit it off immediately. I played "Colonel Godowni" an Arab leader with charm who became smitten with the Dame covering as a CIA spy.

I loved the director George Miller. He was a regular Aussie with a terrific sense of humor. While rehearsing a scene and trying to find my footing, George blurted out, "Lovely performance Thaao, just take three weeks out of it, will you?" He could have said, "Too bloody slow Thaao," but no he did it without ridiculing me and that was the difference in bringing the best out of an actor without having to be a tyrant.

In one of the interviews I did with "Dame Edna" the reporter asked, "I hear this is a great love story. Why do you think Dame Edna fell in love with the Colonel?"

"It was the uniform," Edna responded happily.

I then replied, "Well I think it was the day when she walked into my dressing room with those Joan Crawford shoulders and when I seductively dropped my drawers she fainted."

"Dame Edna" was not amused. You see, she was a bit of a puritan and that joke was below the belt.

We worked together for two months creating a love story that had us laughing hysterically between takes. There was such a difference when Barry was his

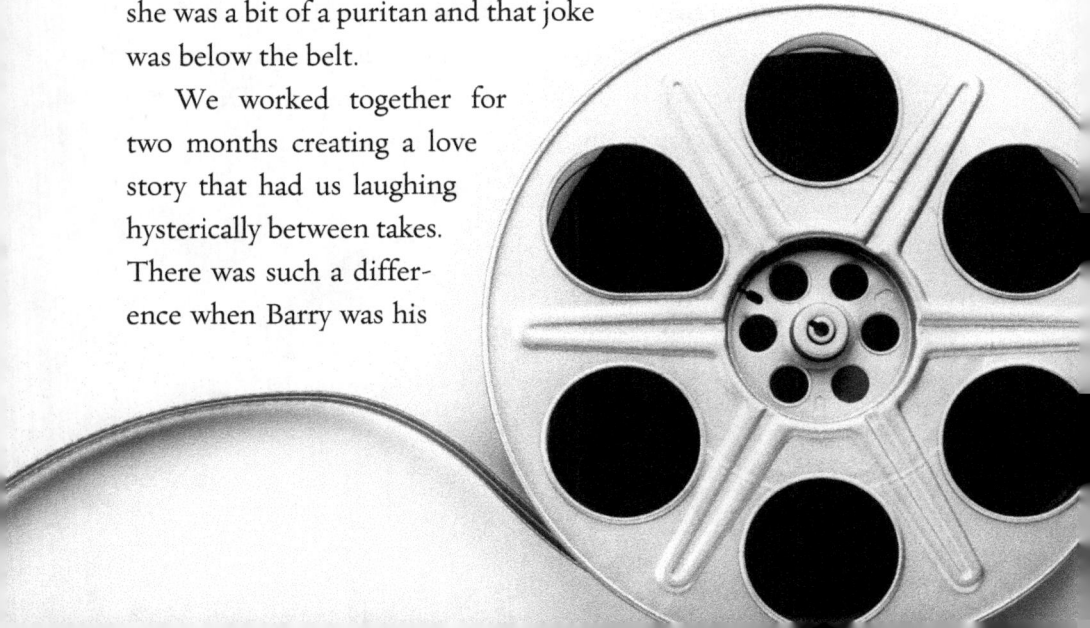

normal self. He was then much more serious and when in character as "Edna" another light shined through.

He kept his alter ego separate, never allowing the illusion to be broken. One day I was sitting in his trailer having a chat between takes when the assistant director came by with his camera and tried to take a photo as Edna was shaving. While still in character, but using his normal voice breaking the fourth wall he said, "Don't you fucking dare!"

It was always important for him to never smash that myth with his public. He had to be protective of that and always on guard. I travelled with him for three weeks all over Australia doing publicity and he opened his door to me. One day he told me that he and his wife Diane wanted to renew their vows and would I be his Best Man? I was very touched with the gesture and gratefully complied. We kept in touch for many years after that and I will still say today there has never been a funnier, more gracious man than Barry Humphries—he lit up my life.

I entertained Barry in my home a couple of times. He was certainly more serious than his alter ego Dame Edna. But that is why it made him such an enigma. He loved art and I remember when he arrived at my house how curious he was investigating my collection. I never knew if he liked my taste but the fact that he inquired about the artist's work was taken as a compliment.

The following is what I served Barry and his wife Diane, the first time they came to my house for supper.

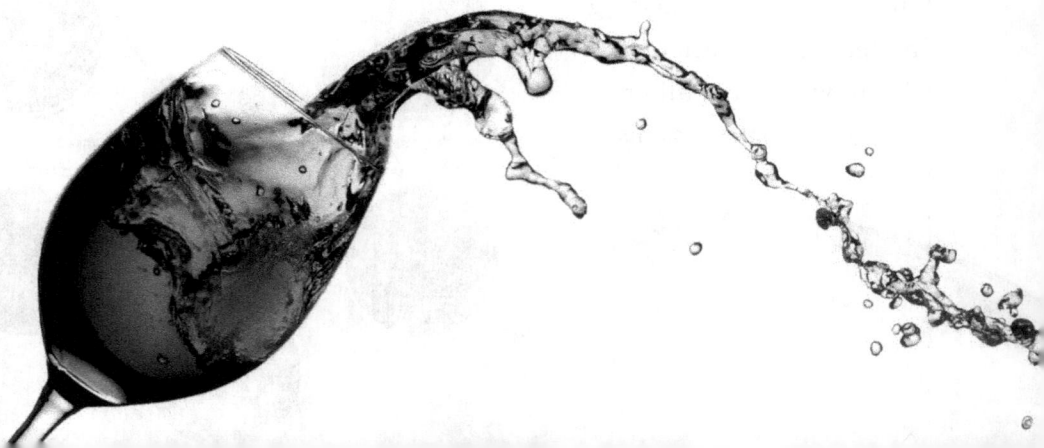

Served over Pasta

INGREDIENTS

4 lobster tails

3 dozen little neck clams

1 red onion

4 ounces butter

3 cloves garlic

salt and pepper

½ cup white wine

1 tablespoon Herbs de Provence

1 pound fresh linguine

INSTRUCTIONS

Melt the butter in a Wok with the chopped onion and garlic. When the onion is translucent, add the herbs, salt and pepper. Wash the clams thoroughly and steam them separately in two glasses of water. When the clams have opened pour the clam juice into the pan adding the ½ glass of white wine.

Cook the mixture for two minutes and add the lobster tails. Cover for 15 minutes. When the tails are done add the clams and toss.

Cook the pasta al dente and place in a large bowl mixing in the seafood.

Serves 4 with an arugula salad and fresh crispy French bread.

INGREDIENTS

1 quart heavy cream

1 ¼ cups milk

1 vanilla bean, scraped

1 ¼ white sugar, divided

10 egg yolks

1 tablespoon vanilla extract

pulp from 6 passion fruit

mint leaves

INSTRUCTIONS

In a heavy saucepan over medium heat, combine cream and milk. Place vanilla bean and scrapings in a pot. And pour in half the white sugar. Allow coming just to a boil.

Next, whisk the egg yolks together with the rest of the sugar and the vanilla extract in a bowl. When cream is ready pour 1/3 of it into the egg mixture, and whisk. Pour egg mixture into the remaining hot cream and return to the heat. Do not boil. Strain custard and chill until cold. Then pour it into a canister and freeze.

When serving, pour the passion fruit over the scooped ice cream and garnish with mint. Serves 4.

With Barry Humphries playing Les Patterson.

In 2015 Barry Humphries/Dame Edna will be doing his last international tour. I will certainly catch the Super-Star before the costumes and disguises take their final bow. He is like no other, which is why he remains a legend.

This past March 2015, I did go to see *The Royal Dame* on her opening night at the Ahmanson Theater and even though her kicks were not as high, she was still at 80 years of age a force to be reckoned with. Her wit was still as sharp as I remembered, the famous lilac hair, the bright costumes and those famous cat's eye glasses all part of her hilarious act, gave her the standing ovation she

deserved. The Dame's boisterous greeting of "Hullo Possums" and greeting those in the upper stalls as "Paupers" along with the "Gladdies" she threw out to the audience at the end of the show to wave them back, finished with a brilliant reveal before the curtain fell when Barry Humphries presented his true self. It was a sad experience for many of us because we knew there never was or will be another like Edna.

I went backstage to see him for my final good-bye, a friendship I would always cherish. It was packed with a lot of celebrities and friends standing in line. An assistant brought me up front to meet Barry as he came out of his dressing room only to be bombarded and pushed aside by other celebrities led by Angelica Huston, Pierce Brosnan and Rosamund Pike and many others. I stood there and watched the game of who was trying to be more important. The cameras flashed as Barry tried to greet his many fans. I caught his eye but the expression on his face was blank. At first I thought did he not recognize me? But as he played his part, with his brief embraces he finally came to me with a hug and a "Hullo Thaao," and that was it. He seemed exhausted going from one admirer to another. I decided not to wait around. I didn't want my final memory of Barry to be a disappointment.

As I walked away with that last experience, my inner self quietly revealed the old adage "That's show-business Baby." After all, isn't life just a memory?

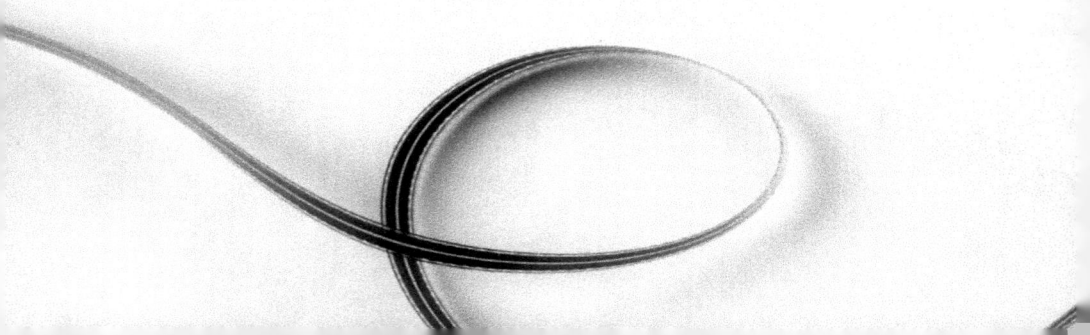

SIR JOHN GIELGUD

Sir John Gielgud from *Much Ado About Nothing* (1959).

ONE RAINY MORNING LILLIAN Gish, the great silent screen star, came into the New York men's wear store named "Meladandri" to buy a gift for one of her dearest friends. She described him as a tall, slim actor and together they would celebrate his birthday in the South of France. She eventually selected a lovely

pale-blue silk shirt that I recommended and we had it wrapped beautifully. She left as she came in, graciously.

Two days later a Rolls Royce pulled up outside Meladandri on 56th Street. Curious, I watched with Roland from the window. A cane popped out first and then a big hat.

"What an entrance," I thought. Must be someone important.

As he lifted his face up I realized it was Sir John Gielgud. And under his arm—unwrapped—was the gift I recommended to Miss Gish.

Roland looked at me and said, "You take care of this one."

Nervously. I went to open the door, but Sir Gielgud beat me to it.

Out came that amazing voice bellowing through the store. "Where's Thaao?"

"Speaking," I said slightly nervous.

"Pale blue?" he admonished.

Facing me was the highly distinguished and prolific performer of the classics, considered to be one of the greatest actors of the 20th century. He was slightly imperious; after all, his accomplishments were immense. And here I was talking to him about a blue shirt. Not quite the same vibration. So I quickly took back my position of awe, and covered it by displaying a number of other colors of the same shirt. He was pleased and chose a navy blue.

While he waited for it to be wrapped he leaned on the counter and spoke

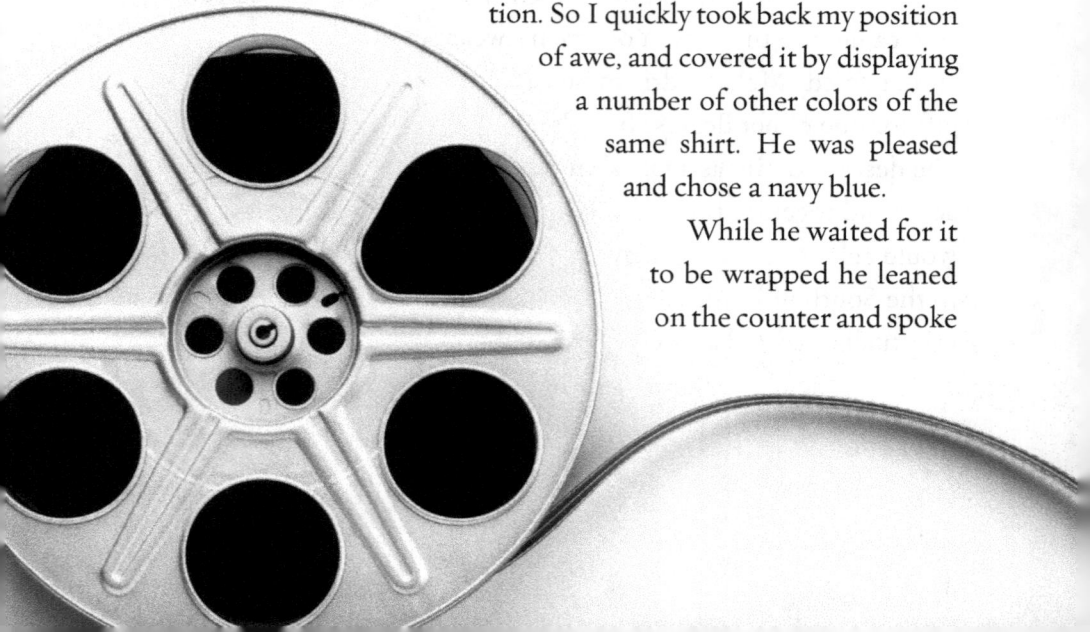

to me like an old friend. I was impressed with his demeanor
when we both finally relaxed and I felt incredibly honored. He
was curious and wanted to know my dreams. When I told him
I aspired to be an actor he said to fulfill that dream I must work
hard and persevere.

"Acting," he said, "was a great privilege . . . you must earn it
and if fulfilled, was a blessing from the gods. Remember perseverance."

He left and I was ecstatic. And so was Roland for my cor-
recting the situation. I was inspired to discover that "great"
privilege and fulfill my destiny through perseverance.

Now that I had lived long enough to remember and com-
prehend so clearly what wisdom he had imparted that special
morning on his way to the South of France to celebrate his
birthday, I imagined, "What would I have served such a particular person celebrating the great work he had contributed in
film and stage?" He had a wicked wit that translated through
his work. His timing was impeccable. I would think his taste in
food was as well.

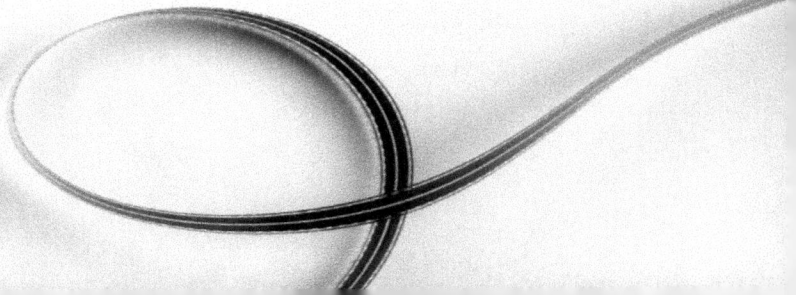

INGREDIENTS

5 cups chicken stock

2 red snapper fillets

5 plump tomatoes

1 dozen clams

1 dozen mussels

1 dozen medium shrimps

10 small-sized squid

1 cup rice

pinch of saffron

1 tablespoon cumin

1 tablespoon curry

¼ pound butter

INSTRUCTIONS

In a large saucepan, heat the chicken stock. Add the rice and cook for 10 minutes. Add cumin, curry and salt and pepper. Then add the sliced snapper, chopped tomatoes and saffron. Cover for 15 minutes.

Clean squid and save the black ink. Slice squid and fry in oil until done. Steam the clams and mussels separately. Place clam and mussel broth into the soup, along with the squid and its ink; and stir in the butter.

Shell shrimp and add them to the soup along with the cooked clams and mussels. Simmer for a few minutes and serve hot with toasted cheese bread. Serves 4.

INGREDIENTS

4 Cornish hens

olive oil

lemon juice

oregano

rosemary

salt and pepper

INSTRUCTIONS

Wash the Cornish hens and dry. Coat with olive oil, then squeeze over the lemon juice. Sprinkle with salt, pepper and oregano on both sides.

Pre-heat oven at 410° F. In a large pan, add 2 cups of water. Place the hen's breast down over a rack. Cook for 20-25 minutes each side until golden brown. It's the intensity of the heat that crispy-browns the hens beautifully while the water keeps the chickens moist.

Serve on a platter with a mushroom or cranberry sauce and steamed brown rice. Serves 4.

Sprinkle with crushed pistachios.

JEN LILLEY

IN 2013, I MET the lovely Jen Lilley on the set for the ancient story of *The Book of Esther*. She had just finished her long run on the soap *General Hospital* and was now moving to *Days of Our Lives*. What made it all so ironic was that I also finished a long run on *Days of Our Lives* and I was about to embark in early 2014 on *General Hospital*. The coincidence was that we were about to both play villains. Well, playing villains, terrorists were nothing new to me. My motto was "I like disturbing happy people." Jen on the other hand never alluded to such a threat. She was so gracious, warm and talented. Jen was to portray "Queen Esther," the Biblical heroine who saves her people from slaughter, whereas

to play "Haman" Esther's nemeses, who plots to kill all of the Jews of ancient Persia. I remember going into a Jewish confectionary in Hollywood after the film and was surprised when someone ordered "Haman pastries." And what do you do with these pastries? You eat them. I found that very humorous.

Lilley was perfect for the part because she had a wonderful disposition, that required her later in the film to show the enormous strength and intelligence needed to beat Haman at his game. The dualities in our characters played well off each other. I charmed the king's court to the hilt until my evil intentions were revealed. Her innocence, beauty and dignity eventually seduced the king and his court. Haman and his ten sons were hanged because of his treachery and the historic Esther saved the day.

I had a hard time playing such a dastardly role, even though I had interpreted villains before. I think it was my compassion towards Jewish people that made it difficult to be the annihilator of this true tale. So I found my own justifications of being so barbarous a character by substituting myself as a holy warrior.

It was a wonderful film experience because there was not one prima donna on the set and our director, David White, ruled a calm ship and always began the day with prayer. That was a first and unique experience in La La Land.

So now that Jen and I are on rival shows what could we share together, certainly not Haman cookies for dessert, but what of the other courses?

INGREDIENTS

1 pound white beans

10 slices prosciutto, pan-grilled

arugula

fresh mint

1 garlic clove

red onion, finely sliced

salt and pepper

olive oil

soy sauce

rice vinegar

INSTRUCTIONS

Soak the white beans in water overnight and take out any discolored ones. In a large saucepan, boil the beans and then simmer. Takes about 40 minutes and then drain.

Mix the beans in 2 tablespoons of olive oil, salt, pepper and chopped garlic clove.

Place the arugula and chopped mint in a bowl. Pour in 3 tablespoons of olive oil, 1 tablespoon soy sauce and rice vinegar and toss lightly.

Add the white beans, prosciutto, and sliced onion to the salad and mix. Sprinkle with black course pepper.

Serves 4.

INGREDIENTS

fillet mignon steaks

black coarse pepper

BEARNAISE SAUCE

2 sticks unsalted butter

4 shallots, finely chopped

2 tablespoons fresh tarragon leaves

4 white peppercorns, crushed

¼ cup white wine vinegar

1/3 cup dry white wine

4 large egg yolks

¼ teaspoon salt

pinch of cayenne

INSTRUCTIONS

Wash the steaks and let sit for an hour.

Heat the grill. Add the steaks and cook for 5 minutes on each side.

BEARNAISE SAUCE

Melt butter over medium heat. Boil shallots, tarragon, peppercorns in vinegar and wine over medium heat until reduced to about ¼ cup and strain into a double boiler. Whisk in the egg yolks. Place the top over the bottom of the double boiler containing simmering water. Wisk constantly. As soon as it thickens slightly, remove the top of the double boiler from above water and continue whisking. Turn off heat. Put the pan of yolks above the hot water. Whisk in melted butter. And whisk in salt and cayenne pepper. Makes about 1 ½ cups.

Spoon over the steak and serve with green beans, and garnish with pimento. Serves 4 with 2 pounds of fillet mignon at 1/2 pound per person.

INGREDIENTS

½ pound butter

5 eggs

¾ cups sugar

1 cup semolina

1 cup flour

2 tablespoons baking powder

¼ teaspoon salt

1 easpoon vanilla

¼ cup blanched almonds

1 jar apricot jam

SYRUP

2 cups water

2 cups sugar

dash of rosewater

INSTRUCTIONS

Preheat oven to 350° F. Grease an 11-inch cake pan. Sprinkle almonds over the pan. Mix butter and sugar well. Add eggs one at a time, mixing well. Add Vanilla and then the semolina gradually and continue to mix. Stir in dry ingredients and beat. Bake 40 minutes.

SYRUP

In a saucepan dissolve sugar over medium heat and boil for 8 minutes. Cool for 10 minutes and pour into cake. When the Rivani has cooled off flip in a serving dish, spread with apricot jam, and cut into diamond wedges. This is one of my favorite desserts.

The daughter of a judge and a director of marketing/ event planner, Jen Lilley was born in Roanoke, Virginia. The thought of celebrating an evening of food and wine as friends rather than the enemies we played, flavorful and down to earth came to mind because of the ancient world we had lived in for that short time. Coming from the South I wanted to share with her a contrast to her youth. Something French, something Greek. In my mind it played out well.

SHIRLEY JONES

When I was fifteen years old in Sydney Australia I went to see the musical film *Carousel*, with my dear friend Joe. The great score of Rogers and Hammerstein's masterpiece moved us both. Those ill-fated lovers played by Shirley Jones and Gordon McCrae has stayed with me my entire life. The memories that

hear that score takes me back to the struggles of my youth and the tragedy of losing my best friend Joe to suicide. It's amazing how music will do that and transport you back to those enigmatic times. I had the pleasure of seeing her in concert in LA, reminding me of those classical films she did in the 50's.

It wasn't until she came to *Days of Our Lives* that we officially met. She was sitting in the make-up chair and I approached her with a smile. She was such a great gal and her attitude was respectful and down to earth. But in 2014, she came onto the *General Hospital* set for a couple of episodes. We bumped into each other in the hallway leading to our dressing rooms. Again there were no airs, just a lovely human whose life, like the characters she played, always sweet and loving. Cannot always say that about some actors who crossed my path. We spoke about tales past including my inquiries about her leading man Gordon McCrae.

"What a great guy," she said of him.

"Actually he was not the first choice for the role in *Carousel*. It was Frank Sinatra playing Billy. We had rehearsed and began recording the album when Ava Gardner, Frankie's great love at the time, called him from Africa while shooting *Mogambo* with Clark Gable. She threatened him, that if he did not get his ass over to the location she would start an affair with another star. Frank got on the next plane to Africa to fulfill Ava's wishes. Now we were looking for another star to fill Sinatra's shoes

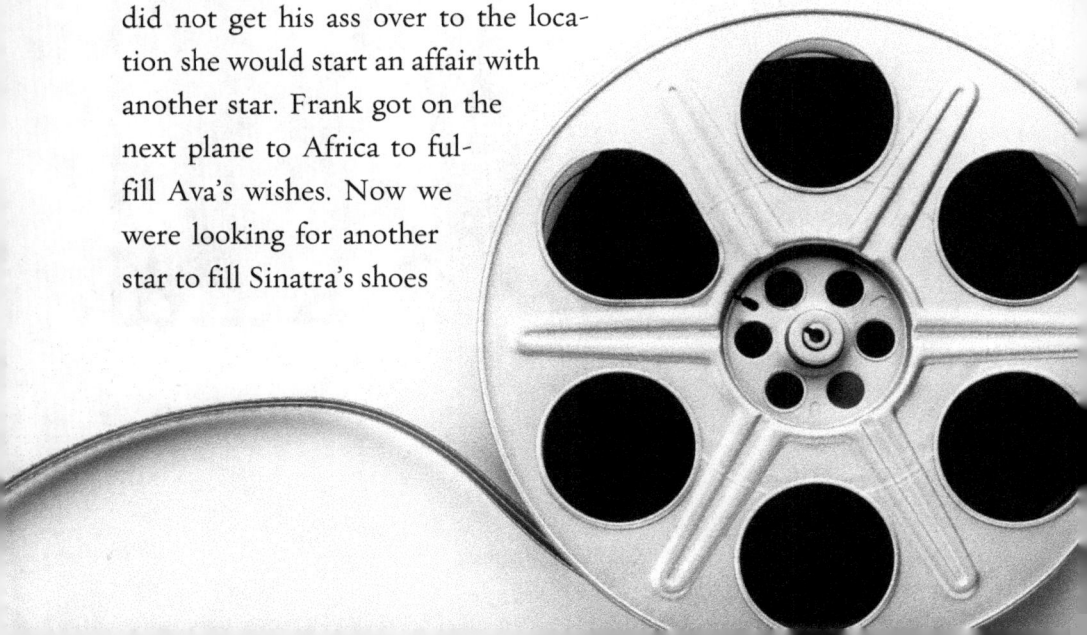

when I suggested Gordon McCrae who she had worked with in *Oklahoma*."

And that's how it became to be, two great entertainers creating another memorable classic. Their first was *Oklahoma*.

From her biography Shirley Jones revealed many women within her. Hardly innocent in her revelations, a very attractive persona and a true artist, she remains a legend today because of those iconic musicals and the Oscar she won as a vengeful prostitute in the film, *Elmer Gantry*. Meeting her again was wonderful. Even my family in OZ saw the picture above and screamed out to me "Shirley Jones?"

One of my favorite dishes is making Baked Clams and Thai Crab Curry that I had created for my 50th birthday party. I've made these dishes many times and was always acknowledged for it. So here it is for Shirley Jones in celebrating her talents and for feeling blessed that our paths crossed.

INGREDIENTS

2 dozen medium-sized clams

1 stick of butter

1 large onion

3 garlic cloves

1 teaspoon white pepper

2 tablespoons finely chopped parsley

½ cup bread crumbs

4 tablespoons sour cream

INSTRUCTIONS

In a large pan, melt half the stick of butter adding white pepper, finely chopped onion and garlic until onion is translucent. Rinse clams and boil in 2 glasses of water until clams have opened. Set aside. Pour the juice into the sautéd onions and stir.

Add the remaining butter and parsley. When butter has melted, add the breadcrumbs to thicken, while stirring in the sour cream for 2 minutes. Take each clam and a shell and place on a flat pan.

Spoon the clam sauce on top of each clam and sprinkle some more bread crumbs on top. Place under broiler for 10 minutes and serve. Serves 4.

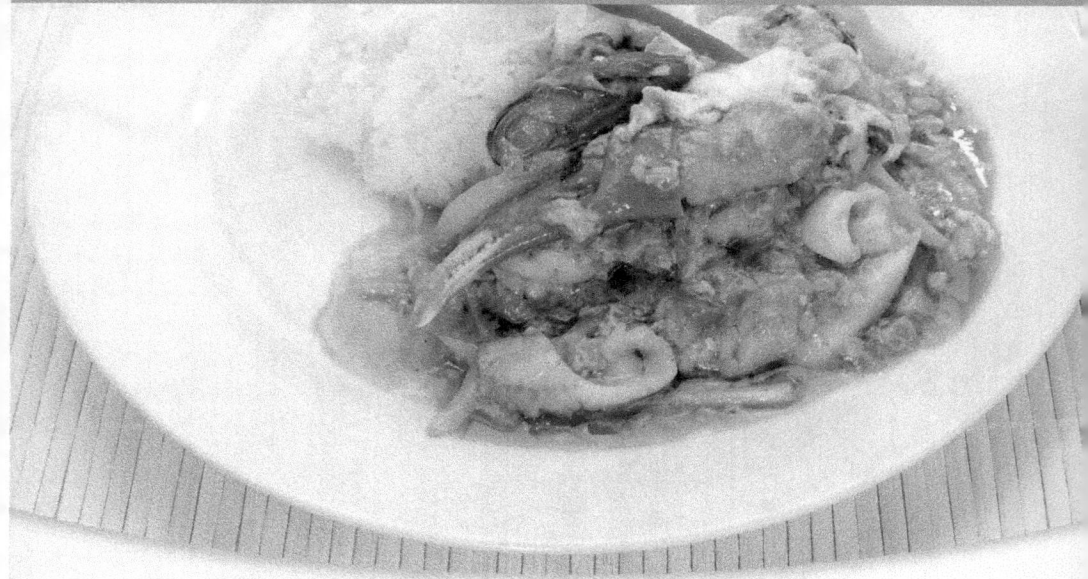

INGREDIENTS

2 pounds lump crabmeat
½ pound sliced calamari
¼ cup of olive oil
2 cups coconut milk
3 teaspoons fish sauce
3 teaspoons honey
4 scallions
8 yellow chile peppers
4 tablespoons yellow curried paste
steamed white basmati rice

YELLOW CURRIED PASTE

8 yellow chile peppers, seeded
½ thinly cut shallots
1 stalk lemon grass
3 tablespoons chopped garlic
1 teaspoon coriander seeds
1 teaspoon caraway seeds
1 tablespoon curry
1 teaspoon dry mustard
1 teaspoon salt
2 tablespoons sugar
½ teaspoon ground cinnamon
3 tablespoons olive oil

INSTRUCTIONS

Slice calamari and fry separately in olive oil. Heat oil in a saucepan and curry paste (See below) until the paste bubbles. Add cooked calamari with the lump crabmeat, coconut milk, fish sauce, honey and the chopped yellow peppers. Stir for 10 minutes and when the crab is heated through place the scallions and mix quickly.

Serve immediately over basmati rice with a green salad. Serves 4.

YELLOW CURRIED PASTE

Combine all the ingredients in a blender until it becomes a smooth paste.

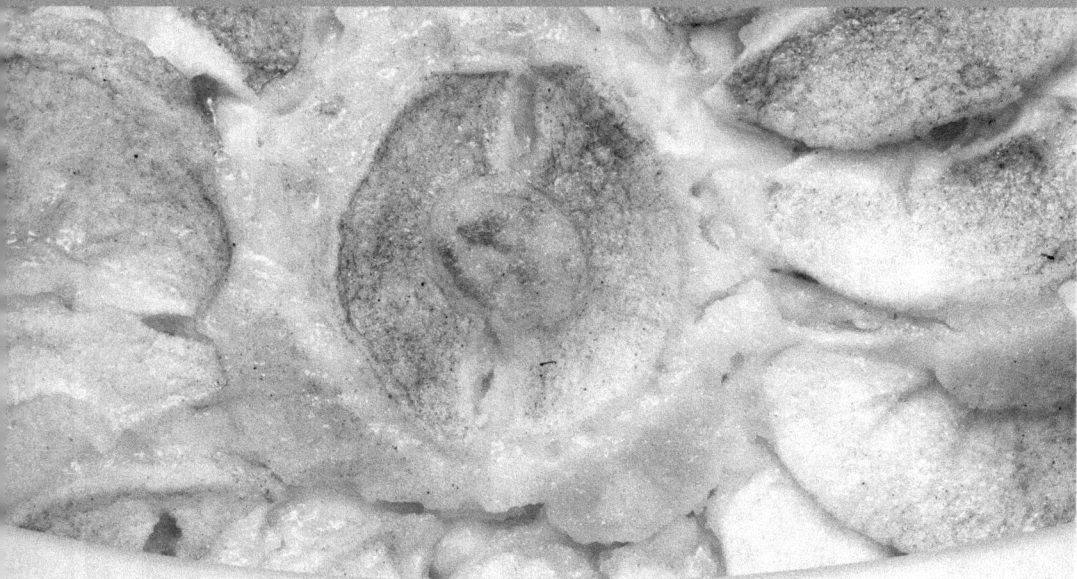

INGREDIENTS

8 apples (peeled and chopped)

½ cup sugar ½ cup water

½ cup butter

1 lemon grated rind

1 orange grated rind

¾ cup of golden raisins

½ cup ground almonds

1 pound pumpernickel bread
with crusts removed

3 eggs separated

½ cup sweet white wine

APRICOT SAUCE

1 cup dried apricot

2½ cups water

¾ cups sugar

INSTRUCTIONS

Cook apples with sugar until the apples are tender. Add the grated peels with the butter, nuts and raisins and mix. In a large bowl, crumble the bread and add the apple mixture. Beat the egg yolks until thick. Beat in the wine and mix into bread and apples. Beat the egg whites until stiff and fold. Grease a 2-quart mold-dish lining the bottom with wax paper and spoon in the mixture. Bake in 350° F. oven for about 1-½ hours. Serves 4.

APRICOT SAUCE

Combine all ingredients in a saucepan. Bring to boil and simmer until apricots are soft. Put into a blender and liquefy. Pour the apricot sauce over the cake and serve with whipped cream.

Shirley Jones is an American icon. She had this larger than life component from the Broadway stage to film and eventually television. America grew to love her as everyone's mum in the series "The Partridge Family," and because of her spirit that she resonated with her family, captivated her audience. She never allowed all that success to go to her head while always maintaining a measure of humility to anyone with whom she'd meet. She simply resonated warmth.

Food is a wonderful way of saying to your guests, "Thank you for being here and I appreciate you in my life."

ELIZABETH TAYLOR

The night I met Elizabeth Taylor.

IN THE EARLY EIGHTIES, Elizabeth Taylor joined *General Hospital* as my sister-in-law as I was being led to prison. I was playing the character "Victor Cassadine." We never worked together as characters but I had the opportunity to meet her at a *General Hospital* benefit. Of course she was always late, the last to arrive but everyone was anticipating her entrance. When that time came for her to enter, everyone stood up to have a glimpse of that amazing myth. Probably the biggest star of her lengthy film career, my castmates dared me to go over to her table and actually introduce

myself. A bet was placed. Nervously I said, "What am I going to talk to her about, the soap? Are you kidding me?"

I was hesitant and afraid I was to be ignored. But after half an hour and being prodded, I approached her table and on one knee, like a true gallant, I introduced myself, thinking "Here comes the bullshit." But instead I was mesmerized by those unreal violet eyes. What a gorgeous broad. At first she was aloof, I smiled and then she smiled back. The door opened. I had fifteen minutes with her and even today I cannot remember any of the conversation because for the first time in my life I was star struck. I wanted to scream out, "It's Elizabeth Taylor?"

Those violet eyes were so seductive that when I got up I kissed her hand, or was it the large diamond ring? She giggled, and I left in a daze. When the other actors who were now envious asked me what we talked about, I smiled gleefully and honestly replied, "I have no idea." But I did it and won the bet.

Taylor did amazing charity work in her later years especially raising money for her AIDS foundation. She had everything in her life except a happy marriage. But she was enormously generous and left a lasting contribution to everything she touched. That's what made her such an International star and great Humanitarian.

I remembered one day getting my hair cut by her hairdresser, Jose Ebert. He told me that he always went over to her home to take care of her hair. But one night at eleven o'clock she called

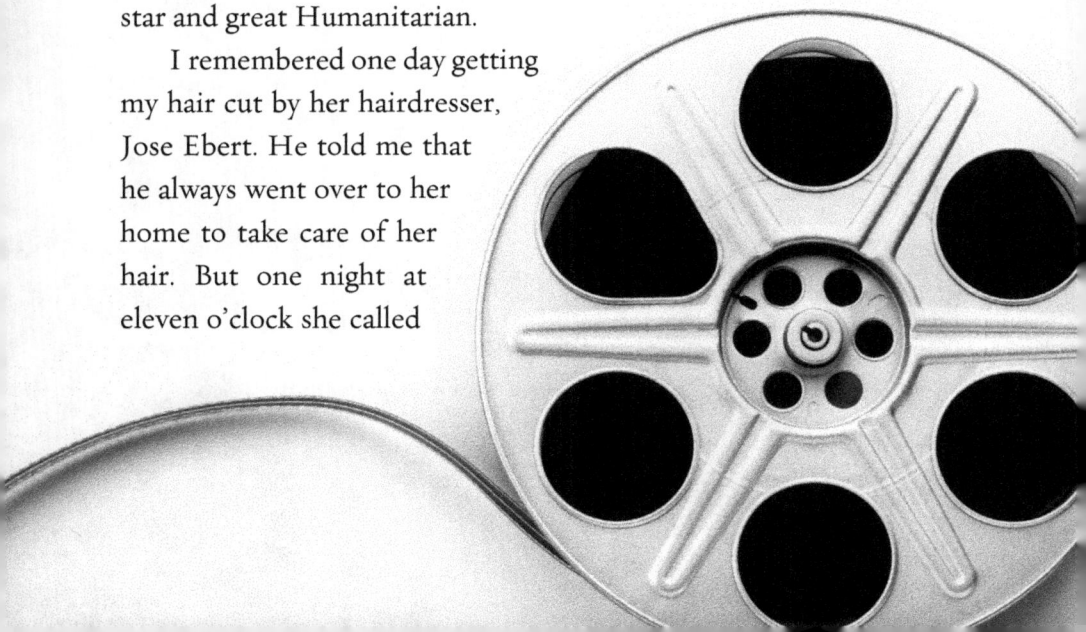

to get her hair done once more. Jose said, "But darling its time for bed. You won't being seeing anyone?"

For which she replied, "I know but my pillow would like it."

Always the star but during her tumultuous marriage to Richard Burton he came home drunk in the early morning hours having shot scenes that day on the film *Anne of a Thousand Days*. My friend, actor John Colicos, who played my brother on *General Hospital* was also in the film. Richard asked him to come back to his hotel room because Elizabeth would be livered for drinking and being out late. The great Burton needed support. When they arrived into his suite, Elizabeth was sitting up in bed looking stunning, holding a handful of dishes which she proceeded to throw at Richard, screaming invectives. John ran out, but on the set the next day Elizabeth was there with her great love, smiling as if nothing had occurred the night before.

There were only a few that stood out with that star quality and she had it in spades. I know she loved her jewels as much as she loved to eat and so now I imagined her sitting at my dining room table with her hair done beautifully, her diamonds shining and that laughter that let you know she was in love with life again. My presentation would have been something like this.

INGREDIENTS

1 pound chicken breast

¼ cup olive oil

2 crushed garlic cloves

2 tablespoons oyster sauce

10 green onions (cut 1½ inch length)

¾ pound of unsalted cashews

mixed green salad mix

INSTRUCTIONS

Slice chicken into thin strips. Heat the oil in Wok. Add garlic and stir until brown. Add the chicken and the oyster sauce and cook for 5 minutes.

Then, add the green onions and cashew nuts and mix together. Place all ingredients onto the mix green salad and serve. Serves 4.

INGREDIENTS

1 duck, about 3 pounds

1 teaspoon Chinese five spice powder

4 red chile peppers, seeded and finely chopped

1 teaspoon brown sugar

1 tablespoon honey

1 tablespoon lemon juice

½ teaspoon salt

1 teaspoon grated ginger

1 teaspoon soy sauce

1 teaspoon sesame oil

2 cloves garlic

2 cups frozen cherries

2 teaspoons orange juice

½ cup water

1 tablespoon cherry brandy

½ cup sugar

INSTRUCTIONS

Rinse duck and pat dry. Pierce the duck all over with a fork. Put all the ingredients above the cherries into a blender until smooth. Rub the mixture all over the duck. Preheat oven at 375° F. Place the duck on a metal rack and add one inch of water into the pan. Bake for one hour and fifteen minutes until the duck is cooked.

Place the cherries in a saucepan with the orange juice, water, brandy and sugar and bring to boil. Stir well. Pour over the duck on a platter and serve with wild wet rice. Serves 4.

INGREDIENTS

2 cups chicken broth

¾ cup brown rice

1 tablespoon olive oil

garlic clove

1 teaspoon cumin

1 teaspoon curry

¼ cup raisins

¼ cup sunflower seeds

INSTRUCTIONS

Place all ingredients in a saucepan and stir.

Bring to boil, cover and simmer until rice is done. (30 mins)

Serve with duck.

INGREDIENTS

1 cup olive oil

2 pounds plain flour

1 cup self-rising flour

2 cups water

SYRUP

4 cups sugar

3 cups water

½ lemon juice

FILLING

1 pound crushed walnuts

½ pound chopped almonds

½ cup coconut

2 cups sugar

2 teaspoons cloves

2 teaspoons nutmeg

2 teaspoons cinnamon

olive oil for frying

INSTRUCTIONS

Bring syrup ingredients to a boil. Simmer for 10 minutes. Rub oil into flour and add water to make soft dough. Knead for 15 minutes until dough is smooth. Divide into 4 portions and roll out thinly. Brush pastry with oil and sprinkle half of the filling mixture and roll up firmly. Cut into oblique pieces (2 inches long).

Heat oil and put the Strava (meaning crooked) and cook for fifteen minutes until brown. Place the dessert into the syrup and leave for 15 minutes.

Serve on a platter. These are my favorite dessert, actually from my mother's recipe.

I wish I did have an evening with Dame Elizabeth Taylor. She was a star that contributed much for all of us. She brought to light issues that many people were ashamed of and feared. She was a faithful individual to her friends and stood by their side when others just whispered. Many awards were granted through her extraordinary life, the last being when she was knighted by the Queen of England. Elizabeth Taylor was a real Dame at last. When she died a few years ago many of the proceeds from Taylor's jewelry auction, which was immense, went to people suffering with AIDS. She was a beacon of light and represented the best of what a star's influence could truly exude. We crossed each other's path but once and that memory has stayed with me through my adult life. I truly hope the menu presented would have met with her approval. I know we would have had many laughs. She was that down to earth.

TELLY SAVALAS

IN THE 1970'S, *KOJAK* was my first acting gig in Hollywood. I was to play a Greek Immigrant, "surprise," smuggling an illegal substance through Ports-of Call in Long Beach, California. Getting off the ship in rainy weather was the perfect backdrop for my dramatic entrance. Perfect for my Greek roots. As I always believed,

"We Greeks, we love tragedy. And why not, we invented it."

Nervous as I was, I always remembered what my first acting teacher "Mary Tarcai" said many times in class, "Use the circumstances you feel into the character your playing, don't waste the emotions, they make it real. It's gold."

It was truly my beginning, a short stint that was introduced in the opening of that particular episode with tragic results. Death was knocking at my door; little did I know that the theme of eternal rest was to remain a constant in the roles that followed. The old acting adage, "Step on your mark and say your line" was executed simply. I breathed a sigh of relief when the director said, "CUT, let's move outside."

I was now a professional actor being paid for my services.

It was four a.m. when I exited Immigration and Customs onto a wet pavement, when a car would screech out of nowhere and hit me hard. As directed, I would be flying through the air, smashing the windshield and die.

My mother would not be pleased. She would think of it as another bad omen.

So now my stuntman was doubling up for me to create this Hollywood reality of action television. When the director called "Action," the stuntman walked in my footsteps while the Chevrolet came racing around, the lights blinding him, before furiously hitting his victim. My character went flying through the air and smashed against the windshield.

"Extraordinary athlete," I thought.

So extraordinary that the stuntman was badly hurt, a broken leg and unconscious. Everyone scrambled around him when within minutes an ambulance arrived rushing him to the

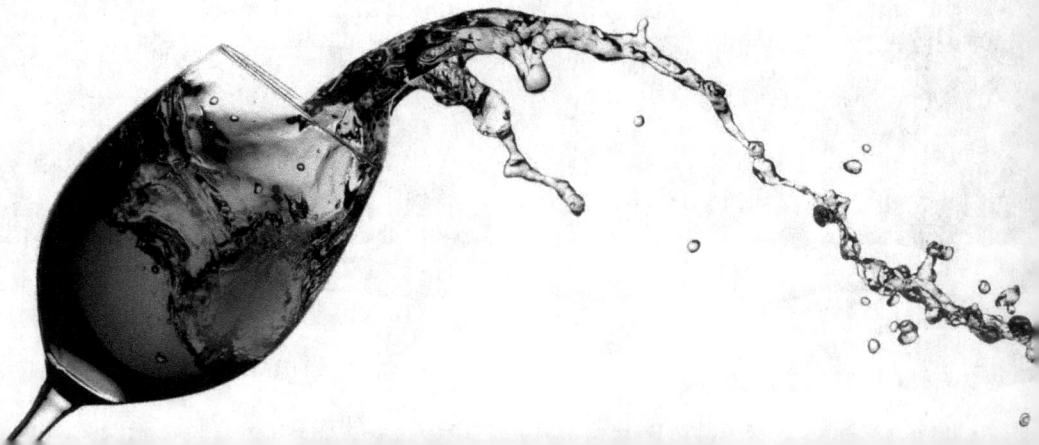

hospital. That could have been me. I was floored when the show had to go on as if nothing happened. Now, I was placed on the cold, wet pavement playing dead, while the technicians lit the scene. It was just five a.m. and freezing when I thought, "This is what it means to start at the bottom."

When suddenly a voice bellowed out, "Are you Greek?

I opened my eyes and there stood the star, Telly Savalas, smiling.

Surprised I said "Yes, sir."

"Get him up," he responded gruffly.

He reached down to me and whispered,

"Would you like a brandy, its cold?" I nodded, "Come to my trailer and we'll catch up."

"Oh would my mummy and daddy be pleased," I thought.

For the next hour we chatted about our heritage. I was quite moved that he was so humble and humorous about the way our history developed in its beginnings for him in America and mine in Australia. We both loved our ancient heritage. There was no "Star" here, playing to an actor in his beginnings, just two fellow Hellenes crossing each other's path.

It would be in the late seventies before our paths would cross again. I was in New York starring in a play called "Jockeys" produced by Jules Stein and directed by Milton Katselas. It was an exciting affair that ended sadly when the play closed prematurely. One

morning I remembered having a dream, so real that I interpreted as an omen . . . .

"To go back to Los Angeles where something important would take place if I left right away." My friends thought I was crazy but I ignored their advice and left for California two days later. Paying attention to that dream changed my life. At the end of that week I was called for an audition for a play called "Play With Fire," at the Geffen Theater in Westwood. Written by Dale Wasserman of "Man of La Mancha" fame. They had already started rehearsals with Victor Buono and Carrie Snodgress when one of the leading actors was fired and they needed a replacement immediately. I was called back twice and got the part of the Grand Inquisitor, a true period of history during the Inquisition in 14th century Prague.

I was beside myself because I listened to my intuition and followed my dream. I loved the experience even though our director, Lee Sankowich, was sick in bed on opening night with the flu. Victor and I got a standing ovation—what an experience that was. To my surprise, one of the silent producers came to our dressing room after that performance. There was a knock at the door and when I opened it to my shock there stood Telly Savalas. He picked up my hand and kissed it. He looked at me for a moment, and that man who picked me up off the ground in Long

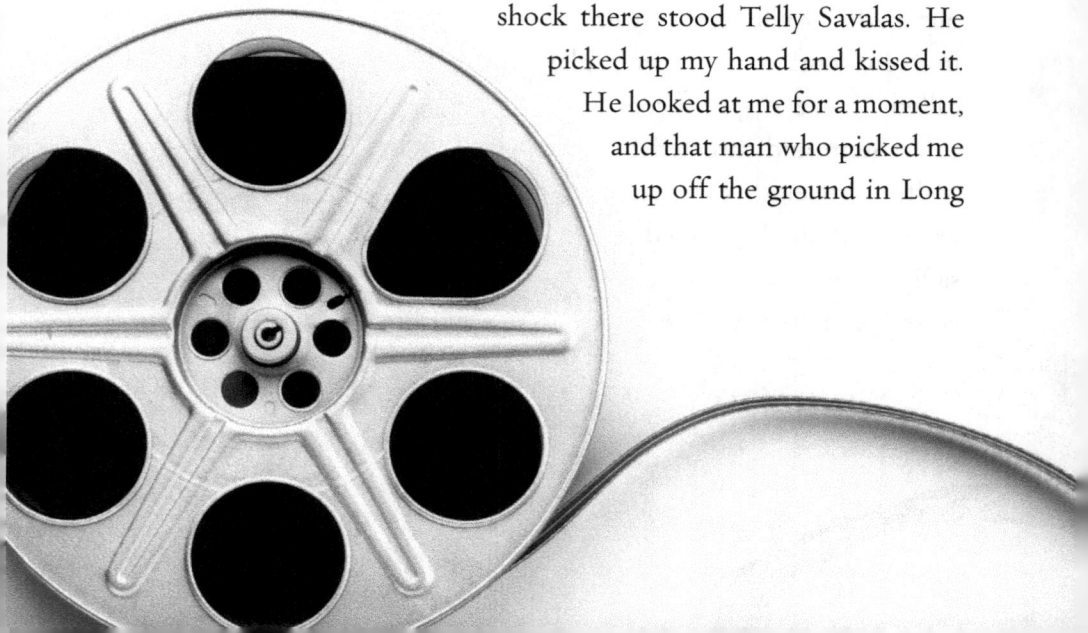

Beach years ago, said, "Bravo, you have come a long way." We had come full circle.

The *LA Times* review came out later that evening while we celebrated. Mr. Savalas read to me: "The play's strongest scenes occur between its most accomplished performers Buono and Penghlis at opposite ends of the spectrum, which account for the sparks that fly when they interact. These are skilled artists who happen to have the best lines."

Telly Savalas always had a grounding presence when he entered a room and when we sat at the table together celebrating life with different types of cuisine; it was uncanny that this lover of great food had as his most famous characteristic "A lollypop."

Sadly he passed away at age 72 of cancer on January 22, 1994, his last Christmas on earth. I can still hear him say, "Who loves ya baby?"

Even though Telly and I had dinner many times—be it Moussaka or Greek Spaghetti or just a simple glass of red wine— he remained a warrior to me. A guy's guy who expressed himself with those strong hands like a Zorba: a passionate, kind and free spirit, whose motto might have been, "This is my life and I don't give a damn." Followed with big hugs.

So I thought outdoors, a fire, a grandmother, relatives, dancing, surrounded by trees with the smell of pine. The answer came, "Animal on a Stick." Pig Roast.

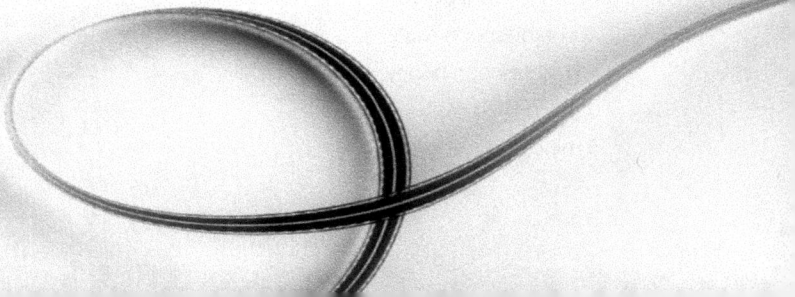

From the restaurant "The Greek Deli" in Melbourne, Australia

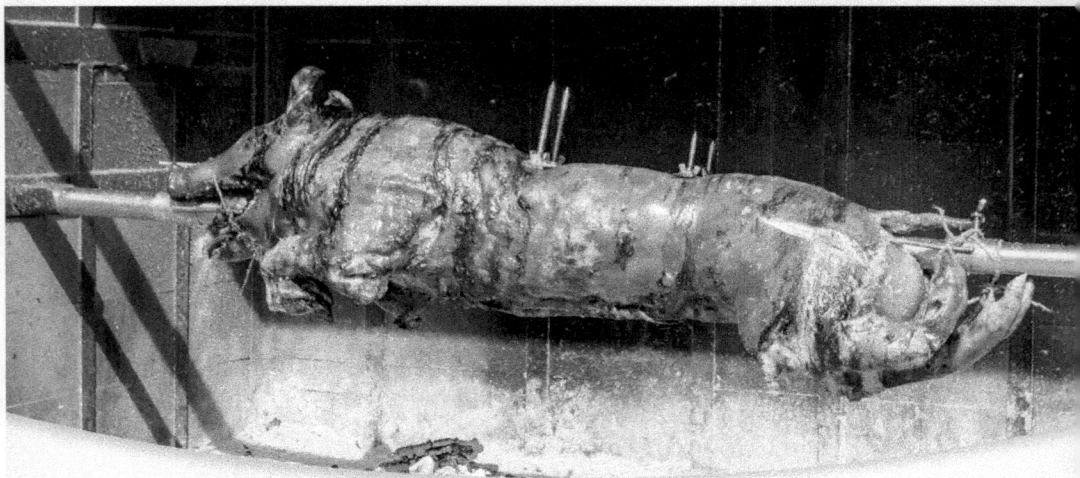

INGREDIENTS

1 piglet

4 long sprigs of rosemary

3 bay leaves

8 crushed cloves of garlic

garlic powder

½ teaspoon grated nutmeg

2 tablespoons crushed coriander

1½ cups red wine

salt and pepper

potatoes

SAUCE (Chinese Cashew and Chile Vinaigrette)

1 cup Roasted chile oil (roast chile and add the oil)

1 1/3 cup Chinese black rice vinegar

1 ½ freshly ground pepper

1 tablespoon sugar

½ tablespoon honey

¾ cup crushed cashews

5 minced cloves garlic

INSTRUCTIONS

After the pig is cleaned and dried, cut inserts into the skin and insert the garlic cloves. Grind the herbs and spices with salt and pepper and rub over the meat except the rosemary and bay leaves that are placed into the cavity of the piglet.

Insert spit and cook for 6 hours turning every half-hour; basting it with the red wine. Place a large aluminum pan underneath the pig with cut-up potatoes, collecting the drippings. The pig is complete when the temperature is 170° F. (approx.) Serves 4.

SAUCE

Wisk all the ingredients in and refrigerate. Serve over the sliced pork and add the potatoes. Serve with a green salad with an ouzo dressing.

INGREDIENTS

¼ cup diced red onion

2 tablespoons red wine vinegar

2 tablespoons honey

1 tablespoon Dijon mustard

1 lemon

1 orange

2 tablespoons ouzo

½ cup olive oil

ground pepper and salt to taste

pine nuts

INSTRUCTIONS

Extract juices from orange and lemon. Add the mustard, honey, ouzo, and diced onion, vinegar and beat together.

Add pinch of salt and pepper and slowly start pouring in the oil. Taste and adjust seasoning for your own taste.

Mix into green salad and serve with the pig.

Greeks love their pastries. My cousin's wife "Christiane Antonas" originally made this for me when I last visited her home in Australia for dinner recently. So I called her up for the recipe of that dessert fit for a king. Telly would have been pleased.

INGREDIENTS

5 egg whites

pinch of salt

1 ¼ cups sugar

1 teaspoon rosewater

1 pound fresh raspberries

2 tablespoons confectioners' sugar

1 ½ cups heavy cream

passion fruit pulp

vegetable oil

INSTRUCTIONS

Pre-heat oven to 350° F. Line two baking trays with baking paper then grease both with oil. Beat the egg whites with salt till stiff. Start adding sugar one tablespoon at a time until meringue is thick and glossy. Pour the meringue mix in one of the prepared trays and lay evenly. Cook for twenty minutes until lightly colored. Remove from the oven and let cool for 15 minutes. Remove and place in the other rectangular tray so that the crisp meringue is on the bottom. Whisk the cream, confectioners' sugar and stir in the rosewater until firm. Spread the cream mixture over the meringue evenly. Sprinkle the raspberries on top of the cream and begin to lightly roll up with the help of the wax paper.

Place in refrigerator for one hour. After, remove the paper carefully, dust with icing, sugar and spoon over the passion fruit and garnish with raspberries. Cut into one-inch thick slices. (Thin slices of strawberries can also be used to garnish.)

In many of my years of entertaining friends and family the ritual of sitting together and breaking bread is an ancient ritual that has been passed down through our families. Everyone's expression has a different outcome but the common thread is the nourishment the kitchen and the host brings to his or her guests. I found that if you didn't love the procedure somehow that resentment affects the food and the energy you serve your friends.

What I remembered about Telly Savalas was how he always appreciated that you took the time to prepare, to embrace and respect him by the way you loved. He taught me how to make a difference.

CHARLTON HESTON

ONE SPRING MORNING WHILE walking along Fifth Avenue in New York City, a tall powerful man with a determined strut raced by me. He was obviously in a hurry. But that was not an unnatural characteristic in a city that thrives on its pace, except for the traffic. But I suddenly stopped as I felt a familiarity about this persona. I started to follow him from across the street and watched other people turning their heads. I was tracking

someone famous. Then it came to me, it was Ben-Hur without his chariot in modern day New York City. I followed Charlton Heston for blocks just to get a closer look at the hero of my teens. He had a strange but powerful gait, although he moved a little like John Wayne did, kind of sideways, leaning more to the right. You see growing up in Australia I had very few heroes to look up to. My mythological heroes were not real, but Heston was alive. And so in the movie theater watching "Ben-Hur" I dreamed of what was and what could be in the private world of my imagination, there in the dark. And here he was walking beside me, off the screen and onto the pavement. Even the score of that classic film brought out the best in my imagination. I wanted to walk up to him and tell him how in my struggling youth I found strength through the heroes he played, but I was afraid to intrude fearing he might reject me and thereby smashing the myth that I kept in my heart. So in a brief moment I came close to touching my hero but out of respect I let him go retaining that myth in my mind of what was.

But years later that was all to change when our paths would cross in Los Angeles and my heart would know that all I suspected was not a lie.

After the play *Play With Fire* had finished its run my fellow thespian, the dear Victor Buono had lost his mother and within months he too passed away from a broken heart. While

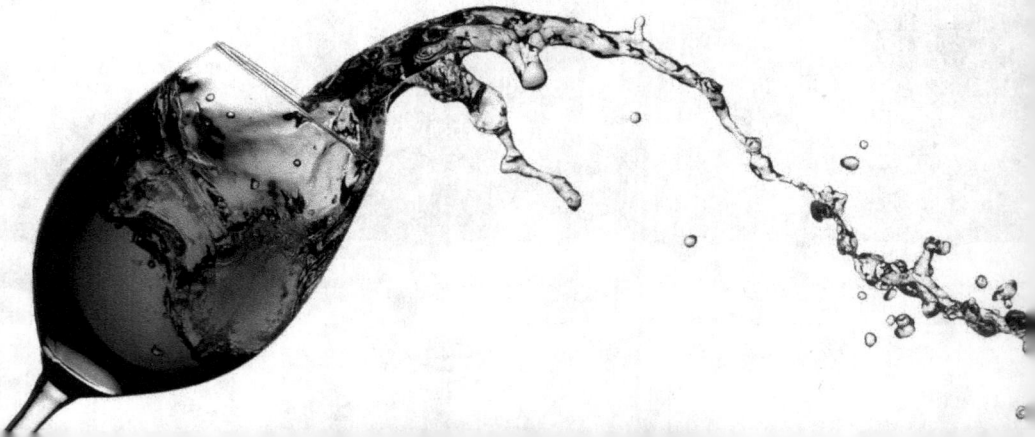

I was in a melancholy mood the phone rang with a request to audition for director Jack O'Brien and the casting director of the Ahmanson Theatre. It was for the revival of the play "A Man for all Seasons" starring Charlton Heston and Vanessa Redgrave. I was beside myself that I could possibly share the stage with the idol of my youth. The casting director had seen my performance and wrote a letter earlier to me commenting on how moved he was by the experience of seeing Victor and me jousting on that stage. He thought I would be perfect for the part of Richard Rich. Knowing how difficult it was in the past to get into the Ahmanson office I was elated and yet nervous in meeting them on the big stage. It was a new step into my career and the possibility of working with Redgrave was also an added incentive.

Surprisingly I did well at my first audition. The feedback seemed promising. After three call backs with director Jack O'Brien I was to meet with Charlton Heston who had final approval. It seemed that I had beat out the competition and now the final step. I have always looked upon Heston as bigger than life because of the parts he played. When I entered the room there was my hero as I remembered him, shaking my hand with a great smile as if to say, "Welcome Son." He was such a gentleman and so supportive when we read together. He truly was there in the present, respectful of our shared performance. I wanted to tell him how I had

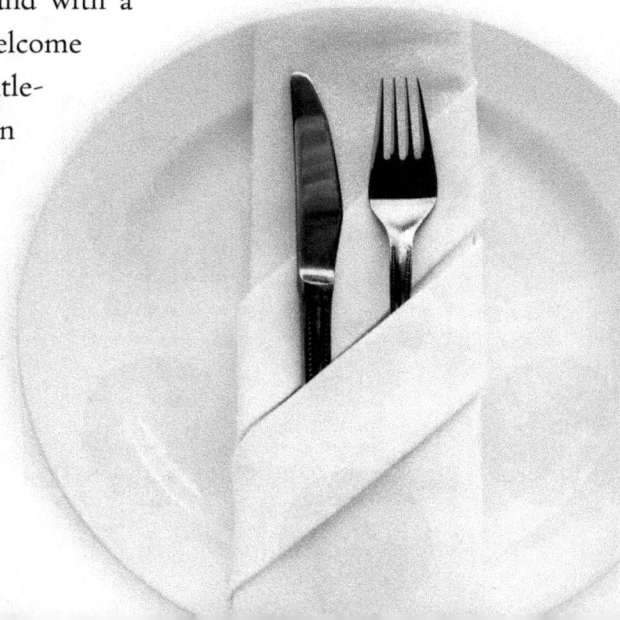

followed him in New York in my youth but I had to behave and retain my mystery. I thought, "This is what dreams are made of." The manifestation of what I imagined in a movie theater long ago.

He commented how much he appreciated the simplicity in my approach to the role of "Richard Rich." It looked like I had the part when my agent got a call that an actor from Broadway—"John Glover"—coveted the same role. As he had already worked with O'Brien I was offered the part of the understudy. Upset, I refused and they threatened that if I did not take the understudy role I would never work at the Ahmanson. And that threat came true. I never did and that person died of a heart attack soon after while sitting on a toilet. Angry and disappointed as I was, life does take care of things on its own.

Years later, John Glover and I studied together in Milton Katselas's class. I told him that story and he was so apologetic, but I wondered what would have transpired in my life if it were otherwise. Three weeks later I got a wonderful role with William Hurt in Ken Russell's *Altered States*. It was not meant to be.

For MY hero, Chuck Heston, I thought I would manifest a feast.

INGREDIENTS

2 pounds black mussels

½ cup water

3 tablespoons olive oil

1 tablespoon soy sauce

juice of 2 Lemons

½ cup white wine

I tablespoon Herbs de Provence

3 garlic cloves

INSTRUCTIONS

Wash the mussels thoroughly. In a deep pan, mix all the ingredients together and toss in the mussels, coating all the shells.

Put the pan under the broiler (approximately 15 minutes) until the mussels have opened, tossing them every five minutes. Discard any unopened shells.

Serves 4 with lemon wedges and toasted French bread.

INGREDIENTS

4 small-sized tilapia

olive oil

2 lemons

fresh mint leaves

fresh sage

tops of celery

I red pepper, sliced thinly

small onion

oregano

salt and pepper

melted butter

SAUCE

1 teaspoon sesame oil

juice from one lime

1 tablespoon rice vinegar

2 garlic cloves, minced

2 tablespoons sweet soy sauce

1 bunch scallions, chopped

1 stick of shaved ginger

INSTRUCTIONS

Brush fish with olive oil. Stuff the belly of the fish with mint leaves, chopped onion sage and celery. Squeeze the lemon juice over the fish and sprinkle over with oregano, salt and pepper.

Place over hot grill for 7-10 minutes on each side. Brush butter over the cooked side to keep moist.

SAUCE

Mix all the ingredients in a saucepan & bring to boil and set aside to cool until the fish is cooked. Pour the sauce over the fish and serve on a large platter over lettuce leaves. Sprinkle with chopped parsley. Serves 4.

Serve with vanilla ice cream. Originally I cooked this for my parents when they first arrived in the United States.

INGREDIENTS

1/3 cup butter

2/3 cup brown sugar

1 ½ tablespoons rum

1 tablespoons vanilla extract

1 teaspoon ground cinnamon

4 bananas (sliced lengthwise)

1/3 cup chopped walnuts

1 pint vanilla ice cream

INSTRUCTIONS

In a large skillet over medium heat, melt the butter. Stir in the sugar, walnuts, vanilla extract and rum. Place the bananas in when the mixture begins to bubble. When the bananas are hot (couple of minutes) serve at once over vanilla ice cream. My parents loved it.

Sometimes I wondered why the Hollywood industry did not acknowledge him in his last years. He made some very fine films and contributed enormously to the history of cinema. Sadly this fine international figure began to lose his memory in the end but the memory of Charlton Heston will always be an inspired one for me, a gracious one, rather than the one he left behind in Hollywood after he died, the image of his arm raised in the air carrying a rifle and saying, "Over my dead hands."

After all this is America, and democracy rules.

WILLIAM HURT

THE MORE I LOOK back at my life and the decisions made, I still wonder whether fate or some pre-ordained schedule had already been established before I entered this complex world, where we seem to know things without justification and yet nothing at all about our true origins. That mystery will never be unraveled in this lifetime; or maybe, just before we succumb, we are given a glimpse of it but then we're gone so that nothing is revealed about the greatest mystery of life. . . . "Where do we go?"

When I made the decision not to understudy at the Ahmanson Theater something else immediately filled its place.

So when I was asked to meet director Ken Russell that helped me travel a different path, was it my bruised ego or was the best choice already prescribed? Because to this day I still regretted the decision with not working with Heston and Redgrave.

The opportunity to meet Russell took place at Paramount Studios in the early afternoon for Paddy Chayefsky's *Altered States*, starring an unknown actor called William Hurt. It was a story of using hallucinogens to explore man's beginnings through an altered state of awareness. When I arrived there, twenty-nine actors were auditioning for the part of Eccheveria, a botanist living in Mexico. Everyone looked the part except for me. I closed my eyes meditating on getting it.

My name was finally called, walked in, shook Russell's cold hand and emptied my props out of a plastic bag, some mushrooms and herbs. I was about to describe the hallucinogens in my opening monologue when the director blurted out, "What's that?"

I said, "My lunch."

"Aren't you going to share it?" he asked.

"What am I, Jesus Christ?" I responded.

He laughed as I continued. I left and as I was walking across the lot the casting director, Joel Thurm, began calling out, "Come back, Russell wants to see you again." I went back for another audition with Russell's direction, and I got the part. I began to work almost immediately on

the Warner's lot and later in Chihuahua, Mexico. It was to turn out to be one of the worst experiences of my life.

On my first day at the studio, I met William Hurt, an interesting but very intellectual actor. He wanted to run lines, and when we did he responded, "Is that the way you're going to do it?" as if questioning my choices.

"Is that the way YOU'RE going to do it?" I replied. He thought me arrogant. We had a not so great beginning.

"Perseverance," I thought.

But as time went on Bill and I got along well and those judgments slowly disappeared. But I will always remember that unforgettable morning, when the movie was to be shut down before it really started. On the first day of shooting with Blair Brown, Bob Balaban and Charles Haid, the actors, decided to be drunk as the script required, only they really were drinking since 7 a.m. I decided with Russell to be the only one sober as a choice and he thought it a great idea.

All was well until Paddy Chayefsky came over to me and whispered in my ear, "I don't know where they found you, but you are exactly what I wrote." I smiled and thanked him, but Russell thought he was giving me direction. Then there was an explosion on the set when the director called the writer a "cunt" and to "leave his set immediately."

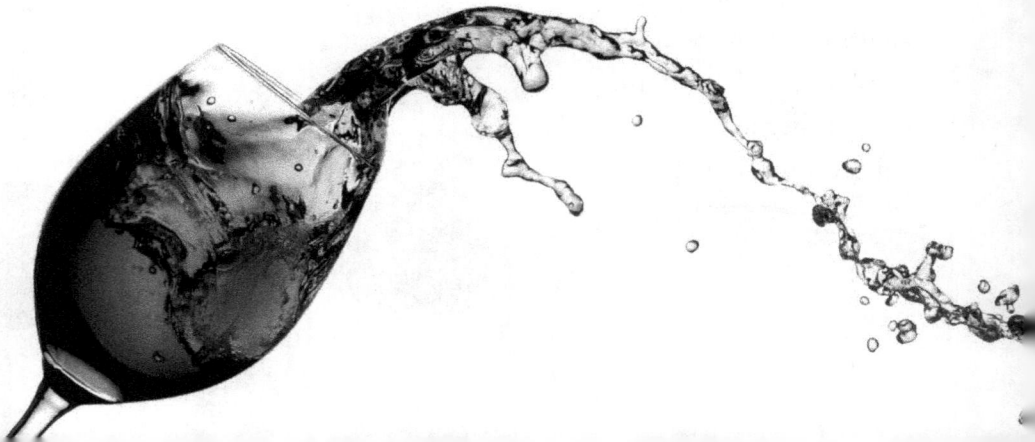

Paddy replied, "You're the cunt" and the war continued until Russell demanded he leave the set or else he would walk. The executive producer tried to intervene but the chaos continued. Chayefsky eventually left the set and took his name off as writer of the film. What a beginning? As the Greek saying goes, "If it stinks in the beginning it smells in the end."

Along the way some of the comments passed onto me was that Russell enjoyed the work exchange between us. He had attacked almost everyone, including Blair Brown. But now we were on top of the mountains in Chihuahua, when after shooting my first scene in Mexico with William Hurt, Russell seemed happy with the progress. While walking along a path he told me how happy he was that I didn't sound like an Australian with that hideous accent. I told him how much I loved his last film *Women in Love* that won him an Oscar nomination. To this day it is still one of my favorite films.

It was a far from peaceful set. Russell began drinking his white wine during work to the point where it got excessive. There was a sequence where two very tall trees that were over a hundred years old were in the way of his shot. He demanded they be cut down. When the Mexican crew did as they were told he dismissed it all as he said the shot still didn't work. He began to be hated on the set and this "madman"as he was being called, was losing control. Due to his fair English skin and too much wine his face began blistering; so I suggested some vitamin

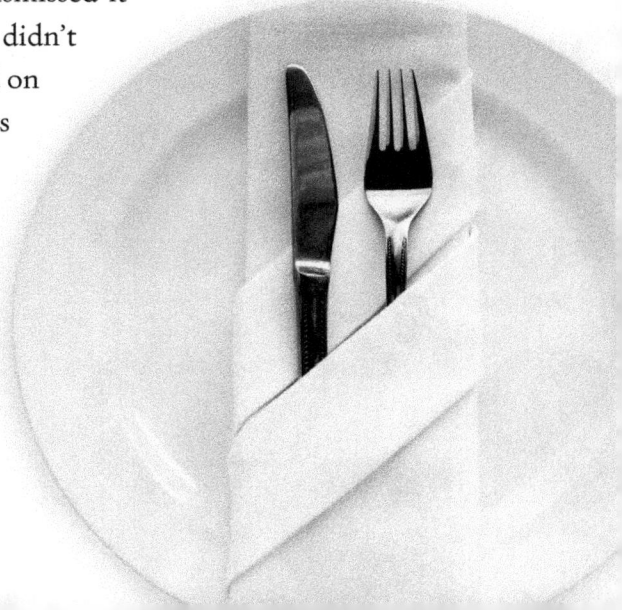

E to keep the swelling down. It helped and he was grateful. William and I continued to work well.

It was an amazing landscape with the indigenous Indians filling in the background. A week later we were on the last scene exiting the tribal area when Ken Russell began cutting our last scene. It was an argument between Hurt's and my response to the hallucinogens that he had taken to expand his mind. I had a full-page monologue that expressed my views on his experience. Now it was being cut in half by Russell, and when I commented that we had all signed a document written by Chayefsky that no dialogue was to be changed without his approval, he just exploded.

"I'm the director here, so just FUCKING do it."

I was stunned and confused as I now lost the meaning of the condensed scene.

The crew set up the shoot in a wide area that was the size of a football field. The camera and Russell were a distance away as they drove toward us zooming in on our conversation. I couldn't remember the lines as I kept struggling with the interpretation. Take after take took place when Russell, who was absolutely furious, came at me with an empty wine bottle.

Screaming his lungs out so all could hear, the director walked towards me with such hate, "Why didn't you tell me you were a fucking amateur?"

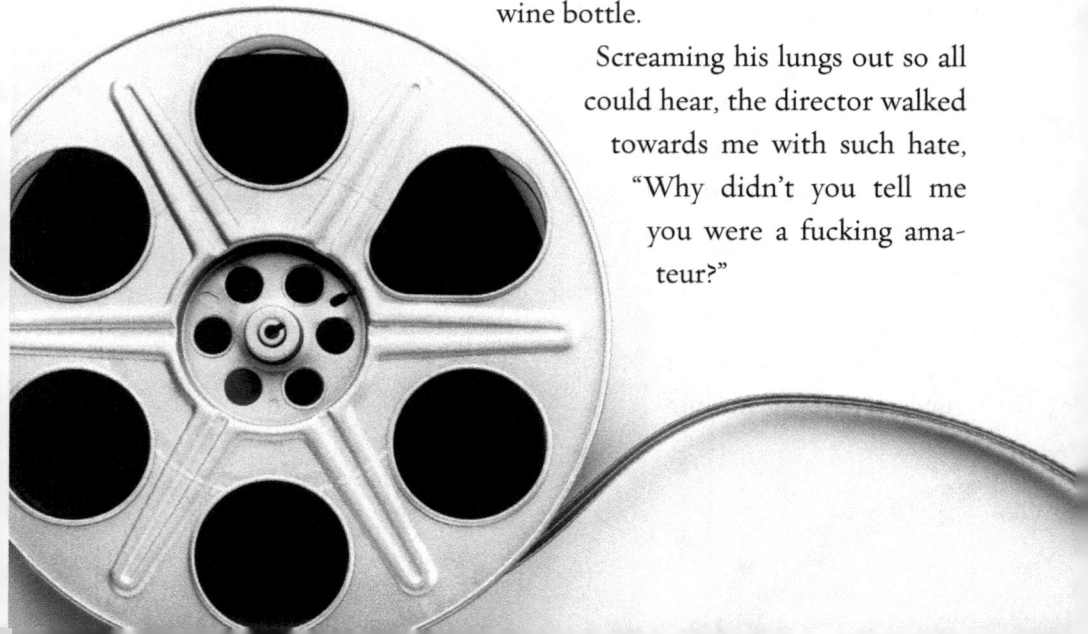

William Hurt moved away when he saw Russell threateningly coming towards me. I felt naked. As he raised his empty wine bottle I stood my ground and thought, "Don't you fucking dare."

I was ready to punch that bloated face if he did. He backed off and quietly said, "Let's try again."

Suddenly, I went into survival mode, and filled with raw emotion, William and I did five perfect takes. When it was over I went straight to my trailer and sobbed my eyes out. I had never been so humiliated. During that last night I was having dinner with Hurt and the crew when Russell walked in with two bottles of Dom Perignon, applauding our work. He sat down with us oblivious to the trust he had annihilated.

With Charles White-Eagle and William Hurt.

The movie was a success and today is considered a classic. Years later while doing *Mission Impossible* in Australia I was asked to host the national daytime talk show with Ken Russell as my first guest. He was directing the opera *Madame Butterfly* in Melbourne. I told my producer at Channel Nine about my experience and his advice was "If he causes any disruption, just cut him off by saying, 'a word from our sponsor.'"

Oh my, a little power over Ken sounded delicious. By satellite, Ken appeared jovial and reminded me what a "wonderful experience we had making the film . . . that Hurt and I were great actors with a job well done." I was so shocked about how nice he was that for the first time since that film, a healing took place. That's how badly that experience had shaken me. Ah, well, drama was his game and I played it with him. He died in November 2011 of Alzheimer's.

Now it was time to get back into the kitchen and stir some pots and flavors of a remembered past.

INGREDIENTS

1 medium-sized octopus

1 cup olive oil

2 large lemons (juiced)

oregano (dried)

salt and pepper

INSTRUCTIONS

Mix the above ingredients together. In a large pot of boiling water dip the octopus 4 times until it's tender but not overcooked. Cut off the head and slice the cephalopod mollusk into 4 sections. Dip it into the oil bath and let sit for a minute and keep stirring.

Baste the grill with oil so that the octopus does not stick. On the very hot grill place the eight sucker–bearing arms and grill all sides for 3 minutes each. In the last minute throw some of the oil mixture over the meat to bring up the flame to charcoal it. When done, take the octopus and mix it back into the oil bath coating it thoroughly.

Place on individual plates and pour over some of the mixture and sprinkle with dry oregano. Garnish with mint & lemon wedges. Serves 4.

INGREDIENTS

1 small lamb (boned)

oregano, dried

garlic powder

4 bay leaves

salt and pepper

olive oil

2 carrots

1 large red onion

8 pita bread

4 Lebanese cucumbers (sliced)

Tzatziki Sauce (see Page 171)

mint leaves

feta cheese

French fries

INSTRUCTIONS

Sprinkle salt, pepper, garlic and oregano over the meat. Pan-fry in olive oil and brown all sides of the boneless lamb. When done, place in a deep pan adding 3 cups of water and chopped vegetables. Sprinkle over the same spices and cover in foil. Cook for 4 hours at 375° F.

Remove from oven, discard foil and let the lamb sit for twenty minutes. Pour the juices over the meat and then shred with gloved hands.

Heat the pita bread. Add the shredded lamb to the bread with cucumbers, mint leaves and Tzatziki Sauce. If you wish, red raw sliced onion can be mixed in, topped with crushed feta cheese. Roll the ingredients together and pin down with toothpicks. Add to plates with hot fries. Serves 4. I first experienced this recipe at George's restaurant in Agios Nikolaos in Crete.

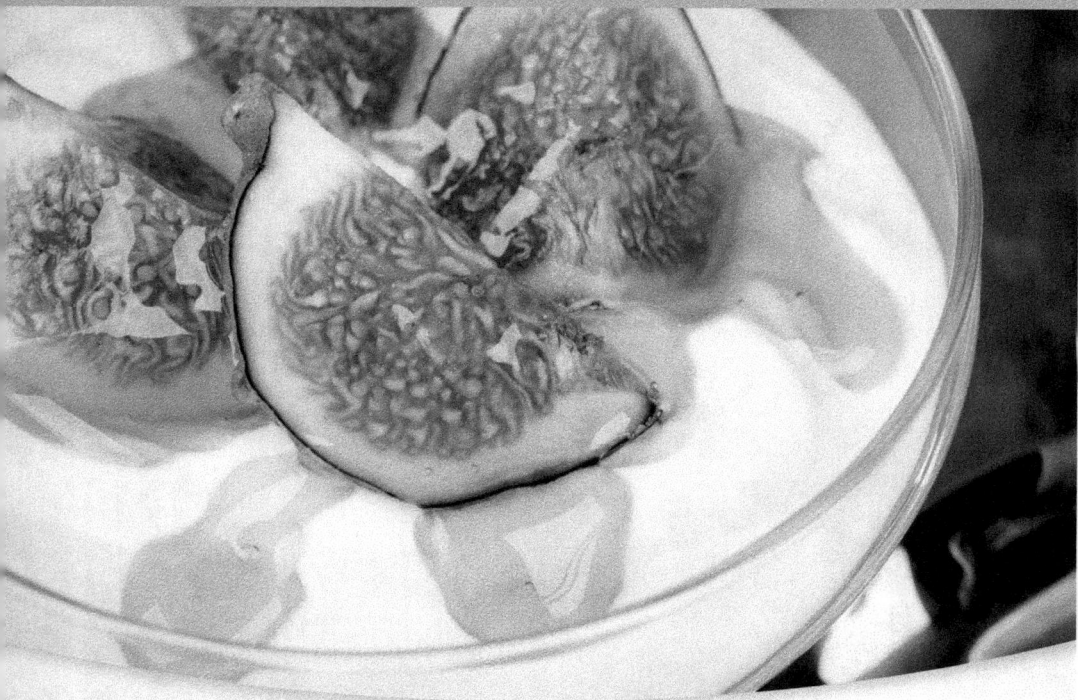

INGREDIENTS

8 large black figs

Greek yogurt

dark honey

crushed walnuts (optional)

INSTRUCTIONS

In individual bowls, add yogurt. Quarter the figs (room temperature), place on top of yogurt and spoon honey over both. As a choice, I like to sprinkle crushed walnuts. It adds to the contrasting textures.

William had invited me to his home for dinner when the filming was over, but I began working in a series and missed that opportunity. We never saw each other again and that is the fate of working in this transient business. You play it as well as you can under the circumstances and see what evolves. It was in my beginnings and his when this experience took place. Tough as it was it had its great lessons to overcome. I am still working as an actor in this unpromising playground, and we know he went on to do great things and win an Oscar. Memories are made of this.

JOANNA CASSIDY

IN THE FALL OF 1999, I received a call from a friend, Australian producer Lynn Bayonas asking for a big favor.

"I have this role Thaao, 'Captain John Brava' in a four-hour mini-series, *Tribe* that I am producing in Melbourne and the tropics of Northern Queensland along the Great Barrier Reef. Modern day pirates seize his magnificent ship and a bloody battle ensues claiming the life of many including the Captain's son. Being a Greek Thaao, you could play that tragedy well," she said convincingly. "Those who survive find themselves marooned on a tropical deserted island, where they band together to ensure

their own survival. The constant threat is the pirates will return to finish what they started. It's a voyage into hell."

How could I say "no," but the only catch was I would die at the end of the first hour and I hated being on the high seas. Like my brother George, sailing was not our greatest attribute. I recalled the time I went out sailing with actor Hal Holbrook during the mini-series *Emma*, throwing up on the deck of his yacht. I thought, "Not again?" When I hesitated, Lynn added how important the part was for the series.

"Think, a Captain of a cruiser takes a group of tourists for an idyllic holiday through the backwaters of the South Pacific, shocking the audience with his untimely death at the end of the first hour. That shock will hook the audience to return for the second half. And your wife will be played by a wonderful and beautiful star, that I cannot reveal at the moment until her contract is sealed."

I contemplated the seduction because that's what it was, convincing the actor to play this vital but small part. I instantly recalled the Australian "Frank Thring" who played Pontius Pilate in my favorite movie *Ben-Hur*. Arriving at Sydney airport he was accosted by the press. One shouting out, "Mr. Thring, Mr. Thring, we hear that you have a small role in the epic film *Ben-Hur*? Was it an important part?"

Thring stopped in his tracks and aloofly responded, "I play the man that crucified

Christ, I would consider that to be an important part," and triumphantly walked off.

"All right Lynn, when do I start?" Lynn was beside herself because she felt that being there gave her a friendship to lean on. A great deal was made and even greater when I was told Joanna Cassidy would play my wife. "Yippee," I thought. You see Joanna and I studied in Milton Katselas's master class for a number of years in the 90's. A stunning actress with a wonderful sensual presence, I knew her only from a distance. But that all changed when we again met in Australia. The connection was instant and we have remained great friends ever since.

In Joanna's kitchen.

Apart from coming from similar backgrounds where the craft was concerned, we both loved to cook and entertain. "Intuitive Cuisine" was how I called it, and sharing that with friends was always a joy in celebrating "Life."

Joanna and I had a great time working together but Lynn stretched my shoot from three weeks to three months. Talk about friendship. The director was George Miller who I had worked with in *Les Patterson Saves the World* opposite Dame Edna. He was a hoot to work with even when on the day as I was contemplating how I should play the emotional through line of our son's tragedy, while taking my time searching, he screamed out, "Lovely performance Thaao, please take three weeks out of it."

He had a great sense of humor and one day he invited me to dinner with Lynn. As we entered his residence he greeted us dancing to the overture of the Village People's YMCA. His wife Connie served a beautiful array of seafood while George sat in his shorts, exposing a lovely image of his protruding belly, full of ant bites. He gave a new meaning to eating in the bush.

One day while shooting in Melbourne I asked him how he saw this character I was playing, as he was not fleshed out well? After a quick thought he said earnestly, "He loves the sea."

"Oh God," I thought. Little did he know that sailing was not one of my talents? So when my ship could not remain docked because of the waves we had to sail out into the heads. I was nervous, afraid to be exposed as a fraud as

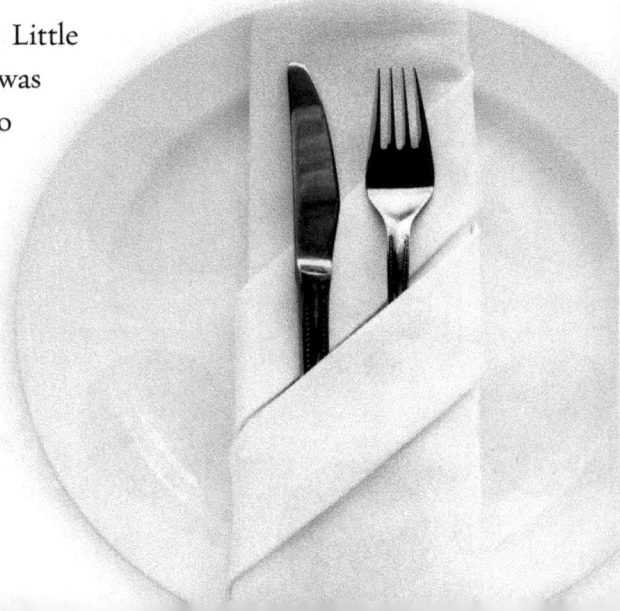

the character was captain of his ship. I hardly felt like a warrior. I kept it to myself but when we entered a dingy and went out through the rough waves the putrid smell of dead fish was all I could bear. When the close-up came I was feeling green. I felt like throwing up but I was able to hold back the lunch. What a little acting can do? It worked, but it took me three days to get my equilibrium back. George was pleased, never knowing the truth.

But with Joanna I felt she intimidated him, "too much woman for this jock," I thought. She had also worked with great actors like Peter O'Toole and Gene Hackman, director Ridley Scott in *Blade Runner* that added to her mystique. George kept his distance and his warmth.

While shooting in the tropical forests of Queensland our individual residences were wonderful bungalows. Except at night when you entered and switched on the light it was not unusual for a giant Huntsman spider to go flying across your face. Joanna always wanted me to enter first just in case. But one day while taking a stroll into the jungle, a giant Cassowary bird that could kill you in an instant crossed our path. Joanna and I froze. It was over six feet tall and it just stood there staring. We held our breath and when it realized we were not a threat it strangely moved on. If we had caught it we could have fed the entire crew. But I remembered a true tale that some explorers tried once. They found out

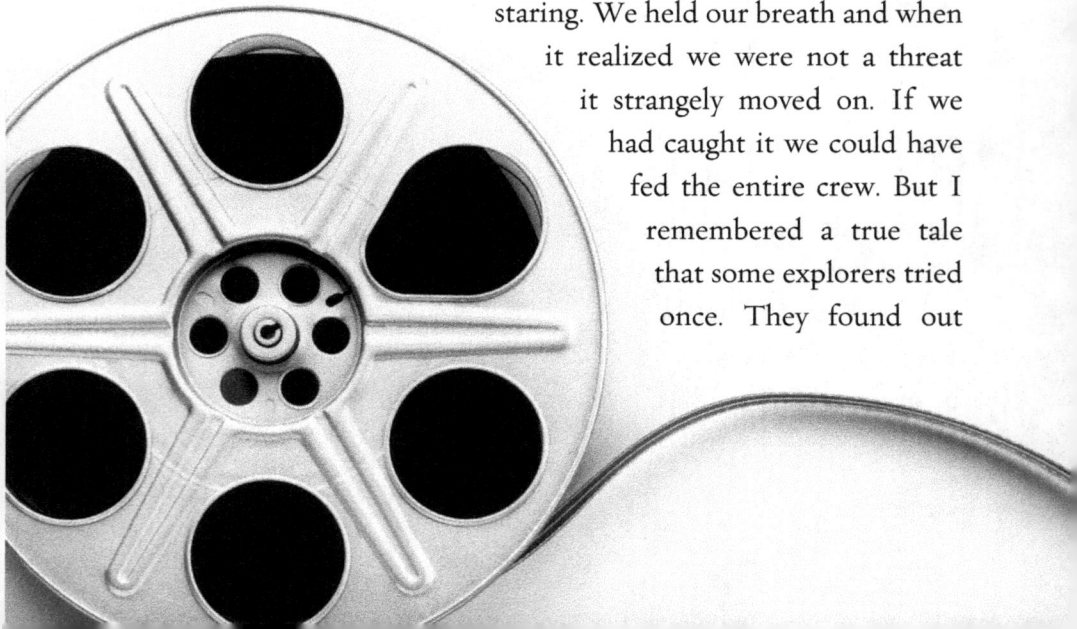

how tough it was. They had been advised after that it "Should be cooked with a stone in the pot: when the stone is ready to eat so is the Cassowary." So much for that cuisine.

The shoot in Queensland went well, even though thousands of giant toads would come out at night, and because it was dark you couldn't help but step on them. The sound was gross; we certainly were shooting in the wild landscapes of Australia. At night we all danced together and Joanna and I let loose to the music. Our great Australian crew I had worked with before on the series *Mission Impossible* in the early nineties would join in making it into a big family affair on location.

We had to eventually fly back to Melbourne and film my death scene, tripping into an animal trap and dying dramatically after falling on a wooden spike. Lynn reminded me again how shocking this death would be for the audience. Ratings were the name of the game. When the series finally aired my boy-scout leader of my youth called to congratulate me, only to remind me I was getting older and obviously playing smaller parts, it was time to come home. It was what I was afraid of but then they say ignorance is bliss. He never did call when the parts were bigger? We never spoke again. He died soon after.

Another death, another tragedy, there is no better way to celebrate life than breaking bread? I took Joanna to my favorite Greek restaurant, Jim Pothitos's "The Greek Deli and Taverna" on Chapel St. in Melbourne. She had never eaten oysters before and now she was about to be seduced.

Joanna was always great company, especially her contagious laugh that was a reminder life was being fully served. Jim

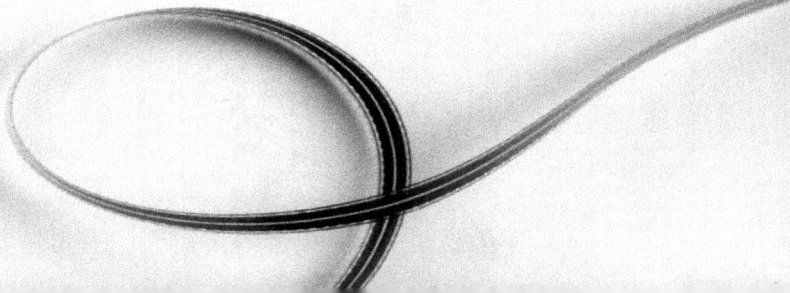

was a wonderful host and always proud of his kitchen. When he presented us with oysters on the half shell with lemon that enhanced its freshness and its smell of the sea. It was the French poet Leon-Paul Fargue who wrote, "Eating oysters was like kissing the sea on the lips."

They lead to discussion, to contemplation and to sensual delight. With a cold glass of Chardonnay, Joanna experienced oysters like it was sex. We laughed and the seduction of food had begun.

Next on the menu was Jim's wonderful way of preparing Octopus. He says, "Ideally it has to be caught early in the morning, tenderized by belting it on rocks, hung out in the summer sun, removed while still slightly moist and charcoal grilled and cut at an acute angle."

His dressing: red wine vinegar, oregano (just sprinkle), freshly cracked pepper and serve with wedges of lemon.

The Octopus that Jim prepared was delicious. When Joanna asked how he was able to keep it so tender without losing its delicate flavor, Jim gave away his secret. "I put it in a washing machine and let it spin for ½ an hour."

"What?" we thought.

Jim laughed at our reaction. "Yes, but I have to get a new machine every year as the old one breaks down."

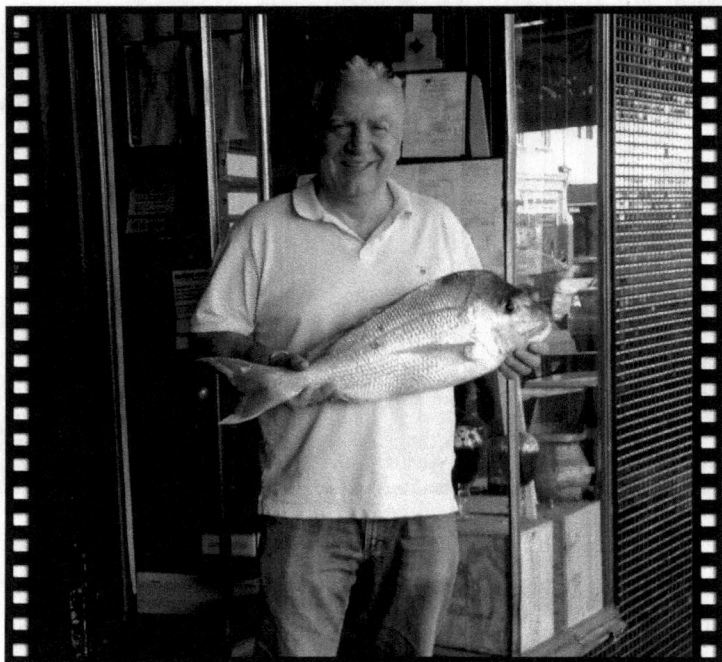

Jim outside his Taverna, presenting his Red Snapper.

It's that magic that brings food to life.

Next on the menu was Jim's Whole Snapper. Prepared simply over the grill and served with a Greek salad of tomatoes, Persian cucumbers and feta cheese dressed with olive oil and balsamic vinegar.

Jim was a source of information. When I asked him what to look at in choosing the fish, he advised, "The fish must be shiny in appearance, scales must be bright not dull, the eyes must be clear not white, and when handling the underbelly of the fish, it must be firm not soft. This confirms freshness and that the fish had not been frozen and then thawed out."

My method was always to lift the rear of the head to check the gills to make sure it was full-blood red. Lastly he said always smell the fish as it must have the beautiful bouquet of the sea. All this preparedness guarantees you a successful meal. Somehow when someone gives you the essence of the food it makes it that much more special. Joanna and I thought so.

We had a great time together sharing exquisite food from Jim's special place—a place inspired by the memory of sitting at

JIM'S SNAPPER MARINADE

INGREDIENTS

EQUAL PARTS:

olive oil

lemon

sea salt

coarsely chopped parsley

lemon rind

INSTRUCTIONS

Make extra to use in the preparation during cooking and when served.

First, scale and gutter the fish and wash thoroughly. Make three narrow incisions from the head to the belly. Using sea salt, rub into fish with some of the marinade. Inside the empty stomach you can place lemon wedges or some coriander. Wrap the fish with glad wrap and refrigerate for 30 minutes. Oil the grill before using and make sure the grill is hot. When the fish is done, careful not to dry out, pour some of the marinade over the entire fish.

If you wish to pan-fry the fish, lightly dust with cumin, flour and lower the heat to finish. Drain oil from pan and add dry rosemary and sprinkle with balsamic vinegar.

Serve simply with lemon wedges and sprigs of parsley. Serves 4.

a down-to-earth fish taverna on a beach at sunset, where traditional seaside village feasts are served. Even today, Joanna and I still talk about it. I remember what the great chef James Beard said, "The secret of good cooking is, first having a love for it . . . If you're convinced that cooking is drudgery, you're never going to be good at it, and you might as well serve up something frozen."

A few days later, I left Melbourne for Sydney to spend time with my family to celebrate another union and break some more bread.

Thank you, Jim and his wife Dora for always being generous and genuine. And Joanna . . . well, we just had dinner again the other evening and as always we celebrated our friendship with food.

JEAN PETERS

AN ARTICLE BY Rick Lyman of the *LA Times* read as follows:

*Jean Peters, a 20th Century Fox contract player whose unpreten-
tious beauty earned her leading roles in some of the top films of
the 40's and 50's before she abandoned her career and practically
disappeared from view after a secretive marriage to the billionaire
Howard Hughes died on October 13th at her home in Carlsbad,
Calif. She was 73.*

A few days ago I went to visit my oldest friends in America
who many years ago introduced me to this beautiful woman

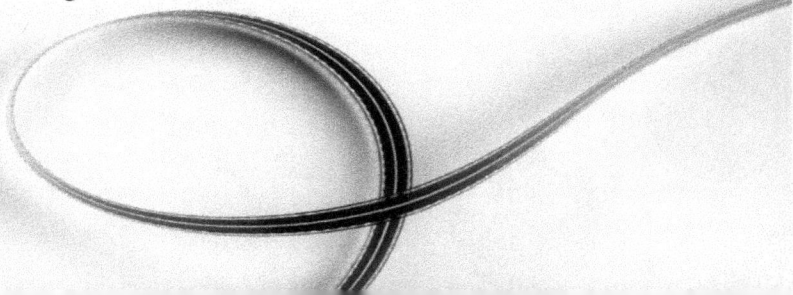

called Jean. Arlen and Schell Stuart were two of the loveliest people you ever wished to meet. Down to earth, humorous, no pretensions, their friendship sincere, I spent many years breaking bread at their dinner table as they did mine. Schell was a producer who had cast me in a pilot and it was Arlen's brother who came into my life when in my youth he walked into the art world I was involved in and said pointedly, "You should be in movies." In a couple of major movies he brought me in as an extra and so my appetite for acting was born.

Today, I specifically went to see them about their great friend Jean Peters who after spending her many years as a major star disappeared from Hollywood to be a housewife to "Howard the mysterious Hughes." Arlen brought out a folder full of Jean's publicity photos and clippings and reminisced about her wonderful friend that she still missed dearly.

After that lovely lunch I drove back home reflecting on how Jean and I had met. Growing up in Australia, I had seen all her movies and remembered what a crush I had on her. That green-eyed beauty, so sensual and straightforward made her a favorite leading lady of some of the top stars of that period; Brando, Tyrone Power, Marilyn Monroe. At 21, she had won a beauty contest as "Miss Ohio State" whose prizes included a Fox screen test. And the rest was history. So when Arlen and Schell asked me over to dinner one evening I walked into their living room in West

Hollywood and there she was graciously extending her hand with a simple, "How do you do?" I kept my calm and she put me at ease right away. She had recognized me from the soap *Days of Our Lives*. I was always surprised when stars had mentioned they were fans. There were no airs when she remarked once, "I don't like servants or big houses and I'm not a woman who likes to play bridge in the afternoon."

As a matter of fact, Arlen mentioned that she and her sisters built their own home. So when she secretly married Howard Hughes and led a reclusive life out of the limelight for 13 years, it was not a surprise to those close to her. Jean was rarely seen in public and never in the company of another man. Her last film was *A Man Called Peter*, with Richard Todd. But my favorites were *Three Coins in a Fountain* and *Niagara* with Marilyn Monroe.

Conversations with Jean Peters.

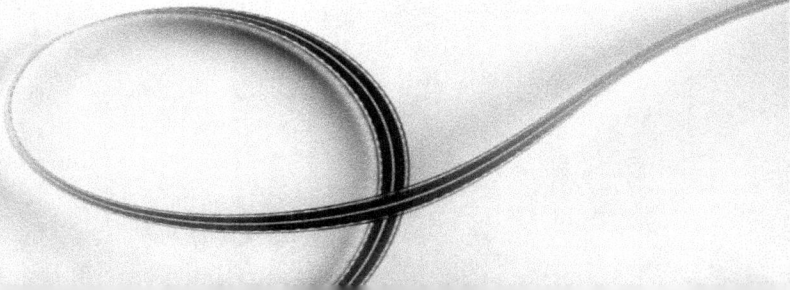

I found it interesting when I read in the *LA Times* that after divorcing Howard Hughes, Ms. Peters had agreed as part of the settlement not to discuss their private life together and not to return to movies, as long as the billionaire was alive.

Peters filed for divorce in 1970. Hughes died in 1976 and Jean refused to discuss the marriage the rest of her life. That's how private she was.

When I met Jean, now married to Stanley Hough, a director of production at 20th Century Fox, I found it interesting that the men she loved in her life were tough but real all-American men, like her, an all-American woman, both steak and potato people. Gracious in manner they recalled their great experiences working in Greece on the mini-series *Peter and Paul*. Stan loved the country especially its cuisine and so I invited them to my home along with Arlen and Schell for a Greek experience. Lamb was what they relished. So I decided to prepare my Greek Mezedes first, followed by my barbequed lamb with a mushroom sauce, served with rosemary potatoes and a Greek salad.

INGREDIENTS

8 large white potatoes

olive oil

fresh rosemary

salt and pepper

2 (24 oounces) racks of lamb

garlic clove

fresh mint

lemon juice

INSTRUCTIONS

At the base of the barbeque, place a round aluminum pan. Surround the pan with two layers of charcoal. Light up and wait 15 minutes for the coals to be red-hot.

Inside the pan, place 8 large white potatoes that have been cut in fours and coated with olive oil, fresh rosemary, salt and pepper.

Make about 6 cavities and place in 1/2 garlic clove and fresh mint, and finally rub the lamb with salt and pepper. Place the leg of lamb on the rack and cook for 20 minutes for every pound. Squeeze lemon juice over the meat about 4 times before it is finally cooked. The lamb drippings and the lemon juice make a wonderfully flavored roast potato.

After the meat is cooked a beautiful brown wait 15 minutes before carving.

Serve with mushroom sauce, potatoes and peas. Serves 4.

INGREDIENTS

½ chopped red onion

2 cloves minced

4 sprigs fresh oregano

and rosemary

salt and pepper

1 pound black mushrooms (sliced)

1 cup chicken broth

4 tablespoons sweet soy

INSTRUCTIONS

Cook the onions and garlic in olive oil and add chopped spices and stir for a few minutes. Add mushrooms.

After 5 minutes add chicken broth and soy sauce and cover on low burner, stirring for 15 minutes. Add to sliced lamb when ready to serve.

Served with Vanilla Ice Cream and Passion Fruit

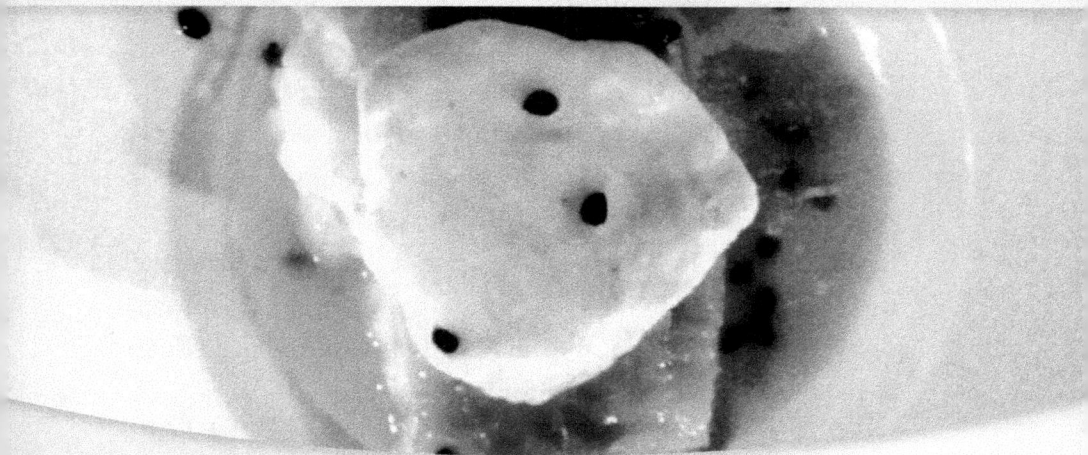

INGREDIENTS

4 cups milk

3 whole eggs

3 egg yokes

½ cup sugar

½ cup fine semolina

2 teaspoons vanilla extract

¾ cup melted unsalted butter

8 oz filo pastry dough

SYRUP

1 cup sugar

½ cup honey

1 tablespoon lemon juice

1 tablespoon brandy

INSTRUCTIONS

Heat milk to boiling point, then remove from heat and let cool slightly. Beat eggs and yokes together with sugar until fluffy and blended.

Add the semolina, blending well. Pour entire mixture into a large heavy pan, adding the hot milk, stirring constantly. Simmer at very low heat, stirring constantly for about 10 minutes until smooth and thick. Remove from heat and add the vanilla, brandy and 4 tablespoons of the melted butter.

Preheat oven to 375 degrees. Brush a 9 x 12 inch baking pan with remaining butter and proceed to layer the filo brushing the butter in between each sheet using at least 6 layers.

Pour the custard onto the filo and smooth evenly, fold in any excess over hanging filo edges. Stack remaining filo sheets brushing each with butter,

Score the top filo sheet lightly to indicate piece size being careful not cut thru to the custard below.

Bake 15 minutes at 375° F. then reduce temperature to 325° F. approximately 35 - 40 minutes until golden brown and crisp.

SYRUP

Add all ingredients to a saucepan, bring to a boil then turn down the heat, simmer for 20 minutes, stirring occasionally. Ladle syrup over the pastry allowing cooling and being absorbed.

Finally cut into squares. Scoop over ice cream and spoon over passion fruit. Serves 4.

After dinner I remember asking Stan what was his favorite thing to do? He responded,

"Screaming at fucking actors."

We all laughed. Jean was always reserved, somehow shy, maybe that was because she had lived with strong men and a cloistered life for so many of her adult years. But Stan loved to talk, dear Arlen always gracious whereas Schell was ready with his funny jokes. It was a great American evening and thank god the food impressed.

Stan Hough died in 1996 and Ms. Peters moved to be closer to her sister in Carlsbad, California.

When Arlen and Schell's daughter got married, I had a chance to see Jean once again. She looked beautiful, still at 72 wearing an elegant white beaded gown. I reached out to shake her hand, when I quickly noticed her enormous ring. I made the embarrassing mistake of shaking her hand too tightly that resulted in her buckling to the floor. I quickly raised her up. I was so upset apologizing profusely. Perturbed for a moment, she pulled herself together and responded with a smile,

"That was a strong shake?"

"Sorry, I mean yes."

"You can save that one for television," she responded humorously.

That was the last time I saw her alive. In the year 2000 at the age of 73 Jean Peters died of Leukemia. Before she died,

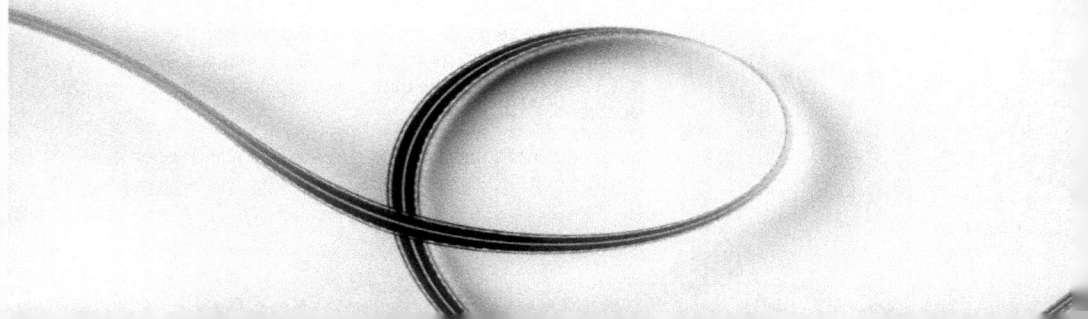

she told her life-long friend Arlen Stuart, "I've had a good life," accepting the fact that she was dying of cancer.

I was invited to go to her private funeral by the Stuart family. It was a simple one for that magical creature I loved in my youth. Some photos were on display from her past history surrounded by a beautiful arrangement of flowers. Some spoke of her life in such endearing terms, especially her sister. My mind drifted off thinking how she played a small part in my life that was special and never disappointing when the memories of some celebrities are best left on screen. Jean still resonates in my mind.

JEFFREY TAMBOR

FIRSTLY, HE IS THE only man I know who was a father and a grandfather in the same week. I look at that face and it makes me laugh. I feel something mischievous is about to happen. A mind that is always deeply curious and why his life and career are constantly being re-invented, and behind that quirky sensitive soul lies a man amused by it all. Which is also why he is a good teacher—he strips things down to the bone to see how it

all works. He gets to know what he is messing with and with economy, finds humor or quietly becomes a killer.

We broke bread many times in Los Angeles. We were both lovers of good food and always interested in trying something different whether it was Italian, Japanese, Greek or I cooking at Katselas's home on a Saturday after class. It was always a fulfilling experience. The circumstances that first brought us together took place at the Beverly Hills Playhouse, at 254 South Robertson Blvd., run by its creator Milton Katselas. We both loved and disliked him because of what he made us look at. It could be raw—his teachings in direction or drama or living life—his was a great influence on many of us. It came alive once a week on a Saturday morning, a master class filled with advanced students looking forward to explore the unknown. And sometimes it bled.

For years Jeffrey Tambor, Alan Williams and I sat in the back of the class giving each other silent gestures that commented on the scene before us, we weren't supposed to but we did. Sometimes we could be kind, after all our business is about the critical. If the scenes were not up to standard and sometimes if Milton felt short-changed, he threatened, and that became a quiet time. God forbid if you had an expression on your face that was derogatory. That would end up being a confrontation. I had a number of those. Alan was always consistently

gracious and one of my favorite human beings. He always sat in the middle of Jeffrey and me. It was fun, professional and at times sobering. A simple eye gesture said it all. We were there to challenge each other, to expand on the freedom that allows our humor to come through and Jeffrey was a champion at that. One time, Jeffrey walked into the class with his nose slightly in the air as he passed by me. I quietly blurted out, "Are we feeling important today?"

He struck his nose higher. How I miss those times. But now Jeffrey has a lovely family with four children since I last saw him. Living in New York with his lovely wife, Kasia Ostlun whom he married in 2001. He even had twins. Somehow this man made good Karma and Karma blessed him back.

Audiences loved him because he created two of the most admired characters in television: the preening and egotistical sidekick Hank Kingsley on the *Larry Saunders Show*, one of my favorites and George Bluth on *Arrested Development*. But he was also a terrific acting coach as he loved actors and his insights were spot on. He lived around actors who were searching and that kept him grounded. In other words, he had lived the life and the perceptions he arrived at shared with his class.

Alan came out of Vietnam, a boxer with a heart of gold. And I of course from Down Under with a mischievous side but we all got along and that's why today we still speak to each other

even though time has shifted and careers have changed. But what I remember while writing this is that in that little theater in the dark we evolved.

One Saturday morning we three decided since we all resonated well, to get together and do a scene for class. The play *Art* by Yasmina Reza, was chosen. So we met for a couple times a week at Jeffrey's house for coffee and rehearsal. Usually scenes in class run about 20 minutes, but we three precious few, decided on an hour scene. Editing a miniature version of the play, we slowly rehearsed over 6 months because all of us had such great fun being together. Jeffrey had a 3-page monologue, and I would take out the *LA Times* reading the latest headlines while he quietly performed. It would get his gander going that I was not paying attention, and he would archly respond, "Are we interrupting you?"

I only did it to stir up conflict. As I knew, I was being rude and found that different circumstances would ignite different emotions when you're exploring a scene. Eventually, we acted our hearts out for the teacher and class on a Saturday morning and got a standing ovation. I remember when we were going to take our bows, I asked Jeffrey if he minded if I came down center stage to take mine. We laughed and then that time was finally over. Milton died five years ago and that was the end of a great era.

In February 2014, Amazon premiered its original series *Transparent* starring Jeffrey Tambor

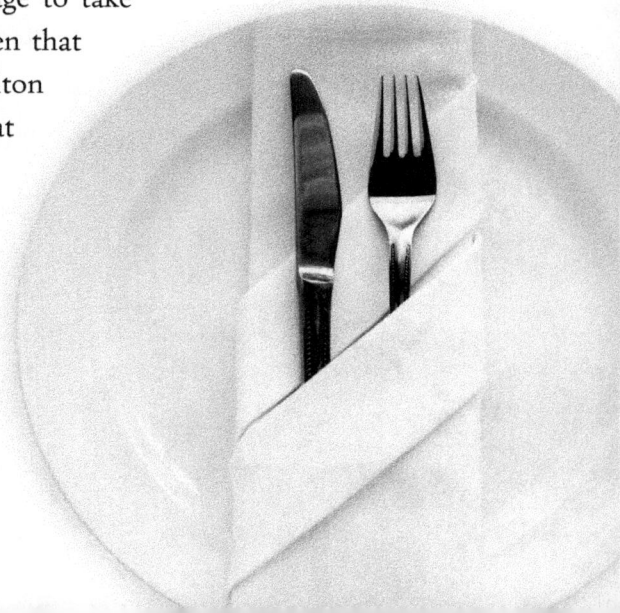

as a transgender, divorced, Jewish father turned mother of three. He won a Golden Globe award for his work and thanked the trans-gender community during his speech. It was not surprising that he would play such a complicated character that could have been a dangerous choice at this stage of his career. But Jeffrey is fearless and that's what makes him such a curious and admired individual. He never settled, and in such a way his success becomes mine through inspiration and not being afraid to live life head-on.

So how to celebrate our connection with a cuisine that he would say on arrival, "For me? I love you." Hugs.

I first tasted these delicious appetizers in Sydney, Australia at a restaurant in Kings Cross. They are easy to make, delicious and unusual.

INGREDIENTS

¾ cup flour

1 teaspoon salt

1½ cups of beer

6 ounces goat cheese

2 tablespoons chopped chives

salt and pepper

10 zucchini blossoms

olive oil for frying

INSTRUCTIONS

Combine flour and salt in a bowl. Whisk in the beer gently until mixture is smoothed out. Cover and put aside.

Rinse the zucchini blossoms gently in cold water and pat dry with cloth. In a small bowl, mix the goat cheese and chives. Add salt and pepper to taste. Stuff a large table-spoon of the cheese inside the blossoms.

Fully immerse the zucchini blossoms into the batter. Discard any excess. Heat the olive oil and fry both sides of the flowers until golden brown. Remove to a paper towel and pat them dry. Serve immediately. Serves 4.

This recipe works well with any firm white fish, tilapia, halibut or cod. It's another fish dish but I remember Jeffrey now with young children and leads a very healthy life. I was taught only to serve fish that has scales.

INGREDIENTS

1 large red snapper

3 thinly cut potatoes

2 brown onions (quartered & sliced)

5 garlic cloves

2 or more tomatoes (medium sliced)

2 bunches of English spinach (roughly chopped)

salt and pepper to taste

1 tablespoon cumin

1 tablespoon oregano

2 lemons thinly sliced

1 cup dry white wine

INSTRUCTIONS

Pre-heat oven to 350° F. Heat the olive oil in a skillet, and sauté the onions. Add garlic and cook for 2 minutes. Salt and pepper to taste.

Add the diced tomatoes and then the spinach and keep stirring for 4 minutes. Turn off the heat. Place the fish cutlets in the baking dish and top them with the wine and lemon juice, followed with salt and pepper, cumin and oregano. Lay slices of tomato and lemon on top followed with the potatoes. Bake for 40-45 minutes. On occasion, pour the liquid in the pan over the fish.

Serve with salad, chopped Lebanese cucumbers, thinly sliced onion and feta cheese, sprinkled with olive oil and oregano, salt and pepper. Papaya sliced into the salad is also recommended. Serves 4.

In our poorer times, my mother would make a spicy, sweet form of an omelet and serve as dessert. I changed it a little but that was where the seed was planted.

INGREDIENTS

1 cup whole milk

juice of one orange

1 tablespoon vanilla extract

1 flat teaspoon cinnamon

½ teaspoon cloves

8 slices white bread

6 tablespoons of plain butter

1 cup melted dark chocolate

INSTRUCTIONS

In a large bowl, beat eggs adding sugar, milk, orange juice, vanilla, cinnamon, cloves and whisk in well. Over medium heat, place a large skillet (non-stick) and add butter.

Dip the bread into the egg-mixture and let soak for 2 minutes. Cook in pan and brown both sides.

While bread is hot, drizzle melted dark chocolate over the slices. Spoon with Greek honey and dust over with icing sugar. Serves 4.

It was great re-connecting with Jeffrey since those old times. Those types of memories are saved when they give you pause. Be it at a diner or a good restaurant we always believed that food was our reward.

I wonder now if Jeffrey's wife, Kasia, when they first met, had she introduced him to a new cuisine from her foreign roots? Having met her I'm sure that in those exchanges, cuisine was indeed prepared to seduce.

TOM HANKS AND RITA WILSON

My passion for cooking started when in my early years in New York I loved being with older people because somehow in life, they had arrived. Their stress was more about the pains and the pills they took for their joints, but always had in common their love for the ritual of eating well. Some were rich enough to have chefs, servants or a butler or some just did it with great style. Sometimes you were invited into their company because they thought you were a pretty youth, maybe a glamorous one, but more importantly that you could carry a relevant conversation.

I watched, I listened and occasionally threw in another opinion, which was sometimes brash because I hadn't yet learned about boundaries. But they persevered, thank god, and many times they laughed. What I did learn about was quality and the importance of timing when it dictated the evening's ritual.

Arriving at Urban Morgan's residence, a wealthy friend who lived on Park Avenue, where precisely at 7 p.m. the elevator door would flow down from the Penthouse and open on cue for the evening's guests. God-forbid if you did not make that entrance on time. Everything had its timing, when firstly Champagne and caviar would be served. Forty-Five minutes later the butler would enter and announce, "Dinner is served."

Just like in the movies, I felt like a kid in a glamorous new playground.

As the evening progressed in that same sophisticated manner, imported French chocolates and Dom Perignon Champagne were served as the final course in the study while playing a card game for four, called "Italian Canasta." At times I felt I was in 18th century France, a bit stuffy, but as an actor I loved what I now realized was a dying ritual. Even my surroundings were embraced by art of the same period and even the wallpaper was 18th century Chinese. Sometimes I was permitted to go into the kitchen and watch the chef conduct his ingredients into a magic formula. It was all about learning to do things well in a society

that lived with the best of everything. Such a contrast to today where so much is expressed through convenience.

Why do I recall all this? Because growing up with Tom Hanks, I kind of noticed he had a bad habit of doing things well. He consistently created magic through his characters and into his true being as a model to emulate. Everyone seems to love and trust this man who never publicly carries any baggage. He has that rare formula like James Stewart or a Gary Cooper had that instantly conjures up trust.

Rita Wilson, his lovely wife, carries those same manners and rituals that we call traditions. And they acknowledge you equally when you are in their presence, "Classy." I call it "Integrity" and shockingly, they also live in Hollywood. So it does still exist here even though you have to discover it through a crowd of stone.

So it was on the 28th September 2002 at the Beverly Wilshire Hotel in Los Angeles, commemorating the 50th Anniversary of the Saint Sophia Cathedral, when I met Tom Hanks and Rita Wilson. I was with Joanna Cassidy that early evening waiting in line to enter the ballroom when Tom and Rita Hanks walked up behind us. Right away we got into conversation as if we were old friends. Rita came from a Greek heritage and when they married at the St. Sophia Cathedral, Tom had converted to Greek Orthodox. The ceremony was conducted by the wonderful and passionate Reverend John Bakas at St. Sophia's Cathedral in Los Angeles on Pico and Normandy.

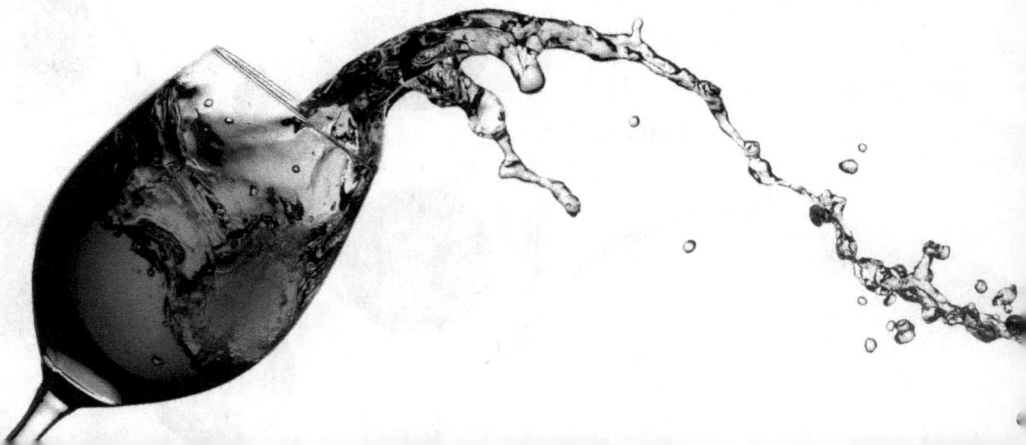

Celebrating Easter at St. Sophia Cathedral

Through the years, the Hanks family have been great con-
tributors to the church. At Greek Easter when Tom and Rita
were in town, they could be found sitting in the front row of
the Cathedral. Tom would also be one of the six carriers of the
"Epitafio," covered in extraordinary flowers depicting the body
of Jesus during the evening's Easter ceremony. They would
walk behind Father Bakas carrying it around the
inside walls of the church followed by
the mellifluous voices of the Greek
choir. It really is a beautiful and
enigmatic ceremony that I
had witnessed every year
since childhood. Though
the sadness of the hymns
brought back my par-
ents' transition I was

always able to recall the beauty of those times when my grandmother taught us the meaning behind those rituals—to be still and respectful in God's presence.

The artists and craftsmen of 20th Century Fox Studios of the early 50's created the extraordinary workmanship of the Greek Orthodox Cathedral headed by Spyros Skouras. This Cathedral was the result of a Hollywood success story. When the Skouras brothers were trying to get ahead in Tinsel Town, they made a vow to God that they would build the most majestic Cathedral if God would grant them success in show business. Their wish was granted and the rest is history. And so the evening of September 28th 2002, we all gathered together to celebrate God in Hollywood with James Giannopoulos, head of 20th Century Fox as master of ceremonies. The whole evening was executed with much pomp and circumstance where everyone embraced the pride of being Greek through the eyes of a celebrated church on its 50th birthday.

Mr. Hanks represents what is best about our industry. Celebrated with Oscars and Emmys through his acting and the producing of first rate and relevant material through television. Even his speeches are always sounds of a moving heart. What a passion he drives. And because of this he is an American icon that will always be a long distance runner.

As for Rita she has had a varied career of her own in acting and producing the most successful

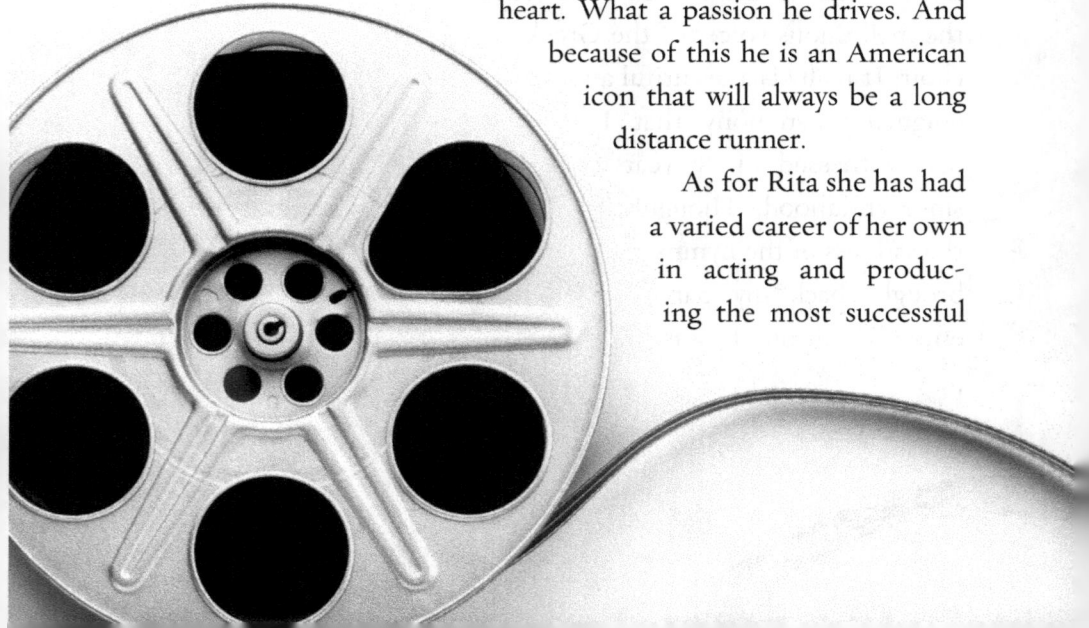

independent movie in American history, *My Big Fat Greek Wedding*. She is also about to open on Broadway in Larry David's *Fish in the Dark* at the Cort Theater.

This past summer we witnessed her successful singing engagement at the Greek Theater in Los Angeles. She has a lovely voice and my party went backstage to see her. Again with no pretense she greeted us like family.

So now it was time to present the menu. I did not want to make it Greek, as that would have been obvious. But as people of the world, I came to see in my mind, "New York Real" with some recipes I had explored when I had lived in that magical city.

Myself, Rita Wilson, Valorie Massalas, Peter and Catherine Georges.

INGREDIENTS

1 pound shrimp

6 cups water

1 ½ stalk fresh lemon grass

¾ pound straw mushrooms

3 Kaffir leaves

3 tablespoons fish sauce

½ cup fresh lime juice

3 tablespoons sliced green onions

2 tablespoon parsley

½ teaspoon red Chile paste

INSTRUCTIONS

Bring the water to boil. Add lemon grass and reduce heat to medium. Add cleaned shrimp and cook for 4 minutes. Stir in the fish sauce and lime juice.

Stir in the green onions, parsley and red chili paste. Finally add fresh mushrooms and chopped tofu if desired. Garnish with parsley sprigs. Serves 6.

With Baked Vegetables in a Chinese BBQ Sauce

INGREDIENTS

1 ¾ pound boneless center-cut pork loin

4 garlic cloves minced

1 tablespoon salt

1 ½ tablespoon fresh sage, (finely chopped)

1 ½ tablespoons thyme

1 tablespoon rosemary leaves, (finely chopped)

1 teaspoon ground pepper

2 ½ tablespoons olive oil

VEGETABLES

2 onions (quartered)

4 carrots

4 parsnips

4 garlic clusters

1 pound asparagus

INSTRUCTIONS

I always take out the meat from the refrigerator and let stand for approximately 1 hour and let sit at room temperature. Preheat oven to 350° F.

In a bowl, combine all the ingredients and mix into a paste. Then rub it all over the pork loin.

Set the pork on a rack in a shallow roasting pan. Add a glass of water to the pan so that the pork remains moist. Add all the vegetables around it in the pan. Cook for approximately 45 minutes, and roll over the vegetables mid-way.

Take the roast out of the oven and cover with foil for 15 minutes. Then slice and serve with roasted vegetables.

Lastly, spoon the BBQ sauce over the sliced pork. Serves 4.

INGREDIENTS

1 tablespoon sesame Seed oil

5 tablespoon hoisin sauce

3 tablespoon plum sauce

2 tablespoon oyster sauce

2 tablespoon Honey

2 tablespoon dry sherry wine

1 teaspoon chile paste

½ teaspoon five spice powder

1 teaspoon minced ginger

1 teaspoon minced garlic

2 tablespoons minced cilantro

2 teaspoons minced green onion

salt and pepper to taste

1 pound sliced shitake mushrooms

INSTRUCTIONS

Mix all the ingredients together and heat slowly in a saucepan.

In a large pan, add 5 tablespoons of olive oil. When heated, add the shitake mushrooms and cook for 5 minutes.

Then add to the sauce and stir.

Having grown up in Australia, fresh fruit was always in abundance, growing wildly over people's fences. So after a full meal, my guests have always appreciated this simple and easy presentation.

Take a quart container of fresh fruit salad of your choice, and one semi-melted quart of vanilla ice cream and combine. Place mixture in a freezer-safe container and re-freeze. Serve with fresh whipped cream.

Just the other day Tom Hanks posted this on Facebook. He always makes his celebrity relevant.

"PRESIDENT OBAMA HOPES TO MAKE TWO YEARS OF FREE COMMUNITY COLLEGE ACCESSIBLE FOR UP TO NINE MILLION AMERICANS. I'M GUESSING THE NEW CONGRESS WILL SQUAWK AT THE $60 BILLION PRICE TAG, BUT I HOPE THE IDEA STICKS, BECAUSE MORE VETERANS, FROM IRAQ AND AFGHANISTAN THIS TIME, AS WELL AS ANOTHER GENERATION OF MOTHERS, SINGLE PARENTS AND WORKERS WHO HAVE BEEN OUT OF THE JOB MARKET, NEED LOWER OBSTACLES BETWEEN NOW AND THE NEXT CHAPTER OF THEIR LIVES. HIGH SCHOOL GRADUATES WITHOUT THE FINANCES FOR A HIGHER EDUCATION CAN POSTPONE TAKING ON BIG LOANS AND MAYBE LUCK INTO THE CLASS THAT WILL REDEFINE THEIR LIFE'S WORK. MANY LIVES WILL BE CHANGED."
– TOM HANKS

As I was writing this episode it was uncanny that this evening is Good Friday for the Greek Orthodox Church. I am sure Tom and Rita will be there in the front row sharing and singing those hymns while recalling what Easter personally means to all of us, to be thankful and feel blessed for that immortal sacrifice. For on this sacred night where Christ was crucified, where the lights go out and the multiplied candles illuminate, our presence is surrounded by gold.

ANTHONY LaPAGLIA

A FELLOW AUSTRALIAN BORN in
Adelaide, our paths first crossed
on *Days of Our Lives* in the
1980's. The first characteristic
I noticed about Anthony

was his great raspy voice. He guested on the show in a two-week arc. He had mentioned that when he saw me in the series in Australia his thought was, "If he can do it so could I?"

So that prompted him to come over and pave his own individual road. And that he did well. In the years ahead, he was best known for his role as FBI agent Jack Malone on the television series, *Without a Trace* which won him a Golden Globe Award. I remember seeing him in his Tony winning performance in Arthur Miller's *The View from the Bridge* on Broadway. That impressed me more than anything else he had achieved, reaffirming his remarkable versatility. Here was a man who made it on his own.

But I need to flash back to the time where we met again in August 1988. I had been called in to audition at Paramount studios for the character of many disguises, "Nicholas Black" in the revival of the series *Mission Impossible*. It went well and that evening I was called back to test. The request from casting was to prepare the two scenes submitted by the next morning. I was very excited as it was to film in Australia because the Writer's Guild had been in an interminably long strike in the U.S. and no new material was permitted. So the producers got around the laws of the writer's strike by using the same written material of the original series from the 70's.

The test took place and I felt positive by the reaction given from casting

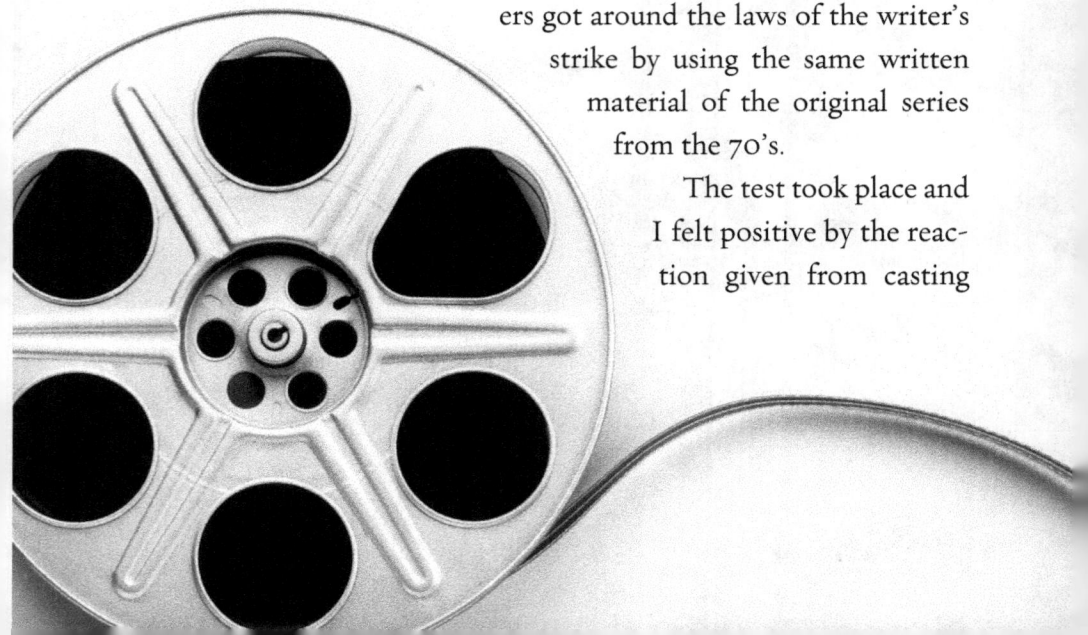

and producers. But that evening I got word that was upsetting. They didn't think it would work out because I came across too glamorous. Besides, ABC had a contract-player they preferred called Anthony LaPaglia. My agent further re-iterated that Paramount had me as their first choice.

"Well that's a positive?"

My agent glumly responded, "Yeah, but I gather that ABC will win out."

I could have kicked his insensitive ass.

"But they still want to see you back tomorrow with both studios present. My suggestion is down play the looks." Right away I thought, "OUTCREATE THEM."

I had to memorize two scenes, one a 72 year-old man and the other a character on death row with twenty minutes to live. Talk about a contrast. I studied really hard that night and that stupid comment by my agent got me out of apathy and right up there into anger. At 8 a.m. I found myself in the Jewish center on Fairfax Avenue in Hollywood sifting through second-hand clothing. I bought an old grey suit for five bucks and a pair of tight old shoes sized ten to affect the walk of the old character. While waiting for my change, I studied the behavior of the elderly walking around me and realized they all had something in common by sharing the same history, "Dignity." That was the hook for me. For the death row character, I chose beating out Anthony for the role that would bring me a life changer.

I arrived at 10 a.m. in my new-old clothing and walked numbingly across the studio like an older man. All the other

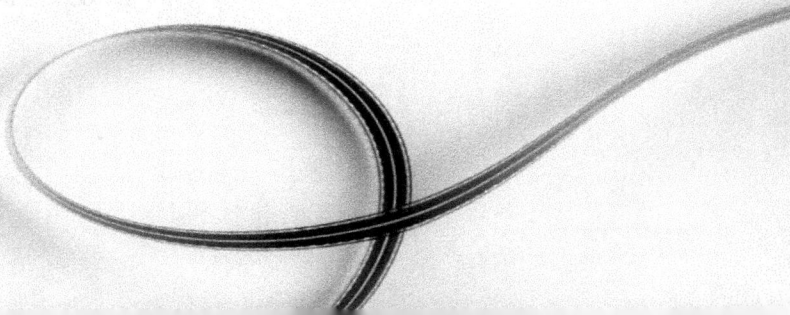

characters for *MI* had now been cast. I put up the "Happy to be there façade" while sitting in the casting office waiting room. Anthony was already there, preparing. Two Australians left, and both up for the same part. We kind of nodded to each other until Anthony said smilingly, "What I went through to get here from Australia and now here with you, up for the same part. Isn't life funny?" He seemed pleased. Which was understandable, his dream was coming alive. I felt like a killer. But who would win it? To me it became a game. I moved away from him to gather my thoughts and work out the obstacles ahead.

My name was called and I slowly walked into the room, which was really like a miniature arena. The Paramount team was on the left, ABC to my right. They didn't seem to recognize me at first as I had put powder in my hair to make it dull and began to create my older man with dignity and transforming into the criminal on death row, hardly glamorous. My rage was furious, and I screamed crying for my life that morning. It must have worked because they all stood up at the end applauding. I was asked to wait. As I went out Anthony asked what the noise was all about?

"I have no idea," was my response.

He went in and played his part. When Anthony came out and he was asked to wait as well. Twenty minutes later the casting agent said we could leave and thanked us for coming. She gave me a wink. Was that a sign?

We made our way to the cafeteria to have a coffee together while discussing how great it would be to go home and play these multiple roles in an iconic series.

Having won that round allowed me to go home to Australia, to my family and the country I left behind. It was a winning experience. I loved the people, I loved the food of OZ and as always still mystified by its rugged landscape.

It was amazing how Australia's diversity with food had changed. Since I left, it had certainly opened its arms to other cultures. My favorite places were going down to the fish markets in Sydney and witness the greatest abundance of seafood I have ever witnessed. To me it was magic time. So I decided to imagine what Gia and Anthony would desire at their host's dinner table?

Or Mud Crab in a Black Bean Sauce

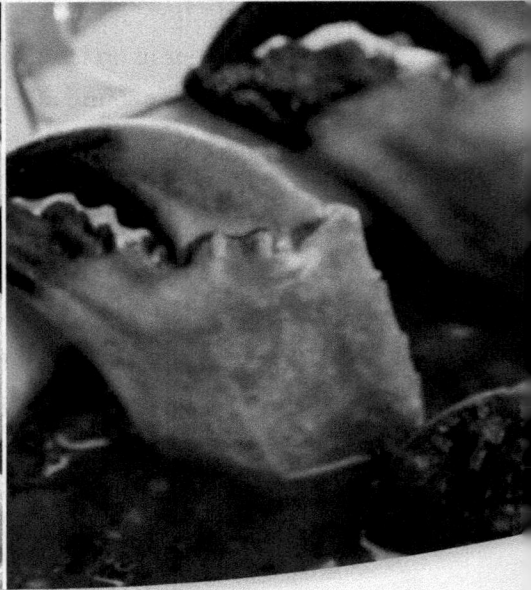

INGREDIENTS

2 large mud crabs (or 4 swimmer crabs to substitute)

3 tablespoons olive oil

4 teaspoons crushed garlic

4 teaspoons grated ginger

2 small red chile (chopped)

½ cup fermented black beans (crushed)

1 cup chicken broth

3 tablespoons Chinese rice wine

1/3 cup soy sauce

1/3 cup ginger (cut into thin strips)

1 cup sliced spring onion

¾ cup coriander (chopped loosely)

INSTRUCTIONS

Wash and clean the crab removing the carapace, guts and lungs. Remove the claws and crack them.

Heat the olive oil in the wok, adding the crabs, tossing them until the shell becomes red. Add the ginger and garlic and keep turning for 6 minutes. Add the stock, black beans, rice wine, chile, onions, soy sauce and cover so that the crab will cook through. Simmer for 8 minutes.

Remove the crab pieces to a large serving plate, including the sauce. Add the spring onions and scatter over some coriander leaves. Serve with toasted cheese bread.

I like serving a Green Papaya Salad after the zesty, pungent crab. Its spicy and crunchy flavor cleanses and leaves the palette feeling refreshed. I learned from the Fijian natives when I lived with them for two months all the possibilities of that wonderful fruit. They used the skin to rub over their faces as a facial, the seeds dried and prepared as pepper, while the meat is also great for nourishment and the digestive system. Serves 4.

INGREDIENTS

1 large green papaya,
shredded finely

1 peeled cucumber and 2
carrots, grated

2 teaspoons minced garlic

1 tablespoon chopped
coriander

1 teaspoon sugar

2 limes (juiced)

salt and pepper

INSTRUCTIONS

Mix the vegetables together in a bowl, adding the
garlic, sugar, coriander and limejuice.

Keep salad chilled before serving.

INGREDIENTS

7 cups of milk

1 cup Half & Half

1 cup of white rice

½ cup raisins

1 teaspoon vanilla

1 cup sugar

cinnamon (powdered and sticks)

1 Fuji apple

INSTRUCTIONS

In a large saucepan, bring milk and cream to a boil. Add rice, raisins, vanilla and sugar. When it comes to a boil stir the ingredients and simmer for 30 minutes or until rice is cooked. Let it sit for another 30 minutes. Scoop the pudding into individual bowls and sprinkle with cinnamon. Put in refrigerator to cool down for a few hours. Add apple slices on top and serve with cinnamon stick.

Anthony was really a nice bloke and very real, and because of that I have always been interested and respectful of his work. I saw him again years later at the Emmys and he greeted me with an embrace and was very open and interested in our changes. We had both survived.

Now married to the wonderful actress Gia Carides, the man from Adelaide had certainly arrived. And my good memories remained. He has now returned back to Australia continuing his good work.

DORIS ROBERTS

WHERE DO I START? How about after 20 years we still study together at the Beverly Hills Playhouse where the late Milton Katselas created in a magical class, "A place of daring." It had great passion and a very curious teacher who manifested our dreams into action, a place where students could safely land. That kind of workshop is gone now. But we were part of something that lived well. So those few of us who stayed and didn't fade from that stage, have remained good friends. And Doris is one of them.

So on a warm, sunny winter afternoon in Hollywood, the wonderful Doris Roberts was sharing stories about her many lives. She sat erectly in her black leather armchair like a Dowager. The life history that started in Russia was facing me like

mother earth, but there was also a strong heart and warmth when she trusted. Through her many experiences she became a true survivor, a long-distance runner, who knew where her power lay. That perseverance gained her many awards including five Emmys and not just from her family series, *All About Raymond*. Doris had also been nominated thirteen times. She wears all this proudly without expectations. It was a career earned.

Ms. Roberts was born in St. Louis, Missouri, to Jewish parents, and knew her father for eight days. One afternoon, she and her mother were standing on the corner of 45th and Broadway in New York. Her mother suddenly announced, "Here comes your father, he went out for a pack of cigarettes and never returned."

Doris was eleven years old when that episode took place.

The father stopped and studied his abandoned child with curiosity, "Aren't you a charmer?"

The young budding actress replied, "Aren't you a bullshit artist?"

A "no bullshit" comedienne with an edge was born.

"Can I take you to lunch tomorrow?" her father said amusingly.

That young daughter had to say "No." She sensed the mother would have killed herself if she had agreed to lunch with that traitor. But Doris always felt it was her fault otherwise why would he have

left? It was her Uncle Willie that saved her. She lights up when he's mentioned. That was the male image she had substituted, without a father there. Someone who watched her, listen to her and loved her. Doris proudly states, "I credit that wonderful man for my greatest achievements. Being abandoned is a terrible thing. It makes it harder to acknowledge yourself when times of embrace, because when it happens, when your innocence is corrupted you spend your entire life trying to grasp what was not there. Thank god for Uncle Willie."

Doris found a way to release through her sense of humor in her work and by the way she can deliver lines like a killer. One of the few left from that golden age of television. She even shared a kitchen with a parrot that swore all the time. Character building, she calls it.

I have been in many quarters with Doris. Certainly the classes kept us current. But sharing food was always a great destination for the two of us. If not at a restaurant, then as I liked to cook my casa was a space she felt at home. It brought to memory the old traditions where the cuisine was created from scratch, where the aromas reminded her "You are family, you are loved." The artistic atmosphere was always illuminated with candles, flowers and a proper table setting surrounded by classical art.

"I feel like I'm having dinner in a museum," she would say appreciatively.

Our great gal also liked playing cards after dinner, especially a game called "Onze."

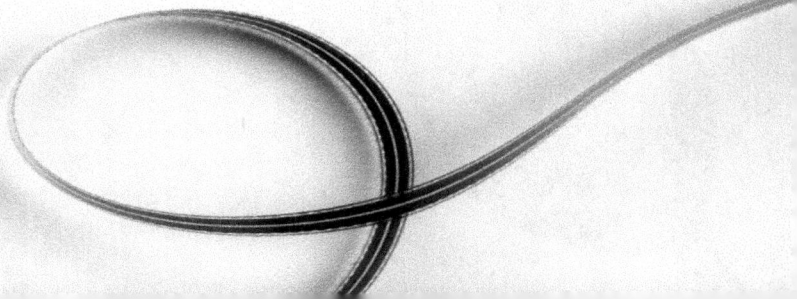

So that afternoon I asked what was her most favorite recipe that she experienced in my home? She was not specific; Doris said all of it because there was always a great ambience created by the guests, the light, the flowers, and the beautiful food. It all came together, it all worked. I think it was the way we explored life in our workshop. We were free to imagine and explore any atmosphere whether it was dangerous or mysterious but it was always innovative. Our minds were allowed to soar.

So I asked Doris what was her favorite food? Without giving any thought, "Italian, just don't serve me any animal innards. I used to cook for my husband William Goyen, wonderful writer, but after he died I stopped cooking. I don't like eating alone," she said definitely, but I made a great Lasagna."

And so when Doris arrived, she always gave a hug and kiss while handing you a bottle of good Champagne. "Open it will you," as she proceeded in finding a comfortable place to sit. That was in the dining area. It seemed that's where most of the guests congregated as well. It was like the old salons where music was background and conversation and food the focus. Most guests never left the table, which was always a good sign. I like to present lots of meze in the beginning as I discovered it would calm the guests in foreign surroundings. The Fresh ingredients used were always a winner, especially seafood or vegetables.

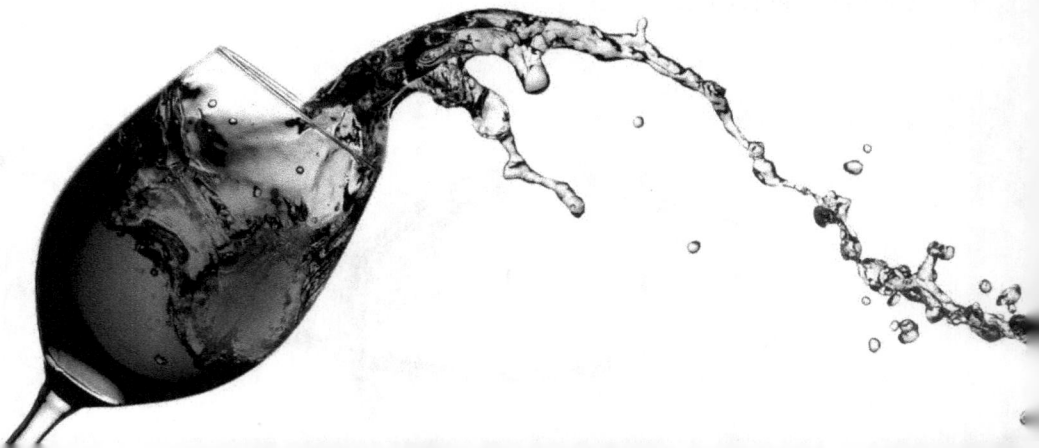

I must say I appreciated having conversations with Doris. She never failed to ask what was going on in your life. And it was not general or shallow conversation to just pass the time. You knew the next time she saw you she would genuinely ask about any changes. Also both of us coming from Milton's class, he always made sure we celebrated our lives no matter how small the success and most of the time we did it through food.

The great survivor whose son gifted her with three grand-children sat back thoughtfully, "I'm in the right place. I feel. Oh, and when you present our cuisine for your book make sure you include that tea you made for me because I got so much better—cleared my chest. I loved it. Pass it on." Done.

Well at least one advantage I thought to getting older, "Finding wisdom."

After dinner, she loved when the playing cards would appear, when four killers would sit for a "Game of Onze." I loved watching their faces when they lost. They took it so seriously. I wondered why as there was no money involved? It was the competiveness of our business that only the strongest survived that bled into the game.

It reminded me of my youth when watching my father play Gin Rummy or Poker with his in-laws, his ears would reveal if he was winning or losing. Red was a good sign whereas white was a warning not to over-step his boundaries. Dad

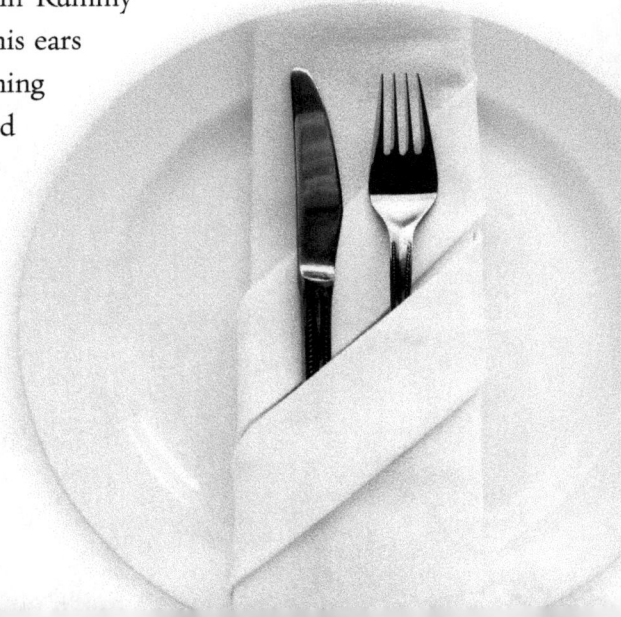

could never keep a good poker face. But we actors did. Pretense was the name of our game.

Now for dinner:

First, a very chilled bottle of Champagne for when the guests arrived.

The Mezedes are already served, including Taramasalada, (red caviar spread) Tsitziki, (yogurt with cucumber slices and spices, Greek olives, feta cheese, spinakopita (spinach pie) and Kefthedes (Greek meatballs).

This is a recipe where in my grandmother's era was understood to be the classic way of making traditional meatballs. They are delicious served with Tzatziki, (yogurt dip). So with Doris we begin with this:

INGREDIENTS

3 white slices of bread
(broken up)

1 clove garlic

1 onion

4 tablespoons fresh mint

1 teaspoon salt

3 tablespoons milk

3 teaspoons black pepper

½ pound ground beef

½ ground lamb

3 eggs

olive oil for frying

all-purpose flour

INSTRUCTIONS

Place bread pieces in a bowl and pour over the milk and set aside. Finely chop the onion. Add it to the bowl along with the meat and eggs, salt and pepper. Mix thoroughly. The women of those days did it with their hands.

Roll into 1-inch balls and coat with the flour. Heat the oil in the skillet and place the meatballs until nicely brown, about 10 minutes. Drain on paper towel and serve with Tzatziki. Serves 4.

With Shitake Mushrooms in Truffle Oil

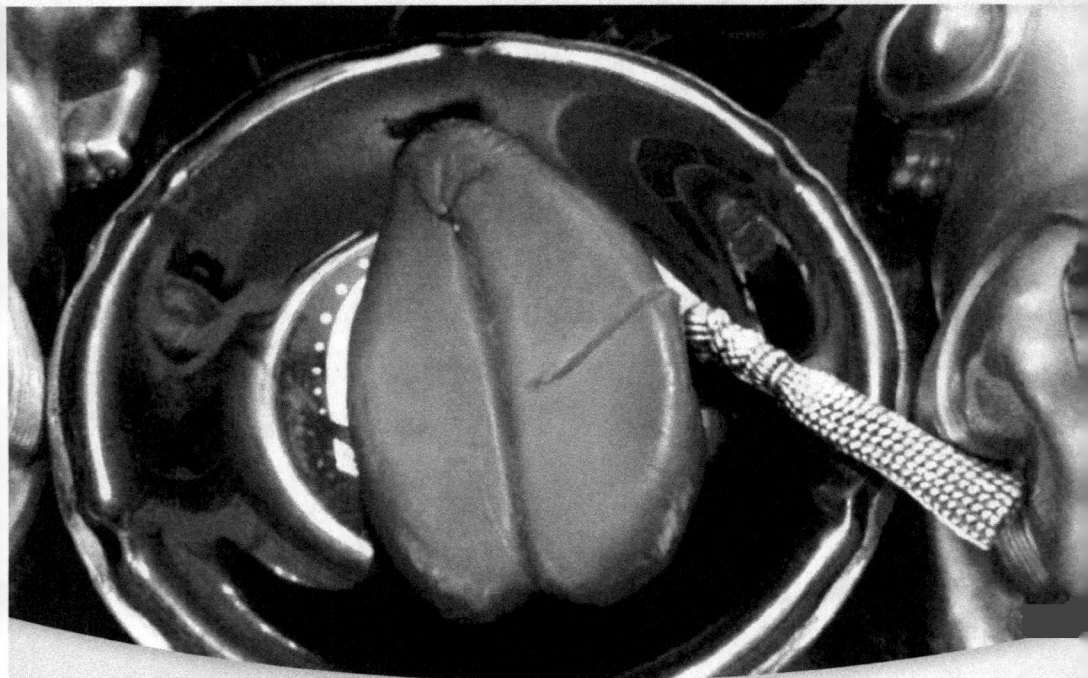

INGREDIENTS

1 pound fresh linguine

3 tablespoons coconut oil

12 shitake mushrooms, thickly sliced

4 garlic cloves

1 dozen basil leaves, thinly chopped

3 red heirloom tomatoes, chopped

1 whole bottarga, thinly sliced

1 cup fresh Parmesan cheese

red pepper flakes, salt

INSTRUCTIONS

Melt the coconut in a frying pan. Add the mushrooms, garlic, salt and cook for 5 minutes. In a saucepan bring the water to a boil adding the linguine and cook for approx 5 minutes, (making sure not to overcook) and drain. Place in a large bowl.

Add the mushrooms and stir lightly, then the basil, tomatoes and raw garlic if you wish. Add the sliced bottarga, red flakes and fold in with truffle oil. Sprinkle with lots of Parmesan cheese. Serves 4.

Toasted bread is always a good partner, but not necessary.

INGREDIENTS

arugula

fresh basil leaves

3 plum tomatoes

10 thin slices of watermelon

5 ounces feta cheese (cubed)

vinaigrette dressing

INSTRUCTIONS

Toss ingredients lightly into arugula. Add the feta cheese. Serve.

INGREDIENTS

3 cups all-purpose flour

¼ ounce dry yeast

½ teaspoon baking powder

½ teaspoon baking soda

½ teaspoon salt

1 tablespoon sugar

1 tablespoon brandy

1 1/2 cups warm water

2 cups olive oil

ground cinnamon and
crushed walnuts

syrup

2 cups sugar

1 stick cinnamon

1 cup water

½ cup honey

INSTRUCTIONS

Dissolve yeast in ½ cup warm water and set aside.

In a large bowl, add the flour, baking soda and baking powder, sugar and salt. Mix well. Add the dissolved yeast, brandy, and 1½ cups water to the other ingredients. Mix the batter for 5 minutes on high speed. Cover and set batter aside in a warm place to rise.

For the syrup, add the water, sugar, cinnamon stick, honey to a saucepan. Boil for 8 minutes, stirring to dissolve sugar. Keep warm.

When the batter has risen, carefully drop a teaspoon of the mixture into the hot (not burning) oil. Turn the puffs over as they turn golden brown. Remove and place on paper towel to absorb excess oil. Dip the puffs into syrup and then roll them into walnuts and cinnamon. Serve immediately. Serves 4.

Doris requested that I serve up this tea and share it with the readers as the broth was magic for her health.

If you feel congestion coming on take these three ingredients, 6-inch piece of ginger (chopped) 1 lemon (halved) and 1 whole garlic and place into a saucepan with 6 cups of water. Bring to a boil and simmer for 30 minutes. Add honey to taste.

It is a great and healthy tea given to me by a Vietnamese doctor. The ginger opens the paws, the lemon cleanses and the garlic heals. It's a perfect triangle. Enjoy.

Doris Roberts remains a wonderful and appreciative friend. Recently, I picked her up and took her to Chinatown in LA just to break the monotony of habit. I held her hand as we walked slowly to the restaurant. There is a wonderful moment that you arrive in life when someone's hand reveals the trust developed through the years. She felt it for those two hours when we went out of town for a new experience. I even took her to a Chinese ice-cream parlor for a flavor of chocolate. She was like an innocent child, like daddy was there again. The food was different from what she was used to and that in itself was a new discovery. A change that allowed her to feel, "I am not dead yet." Her curiosity has kept her alive, even for all those trophies and awards that still sit on the shelves of her house, it was affection and good company that brought real meaning to this stage of her life. She still wanted to be loved, to be held even by a kind voice. I realized at that moment we begin as children and then come full circle to be a child once again. Somehow that ice cream brought out her innocence.

What is in the beginning is also in the end.

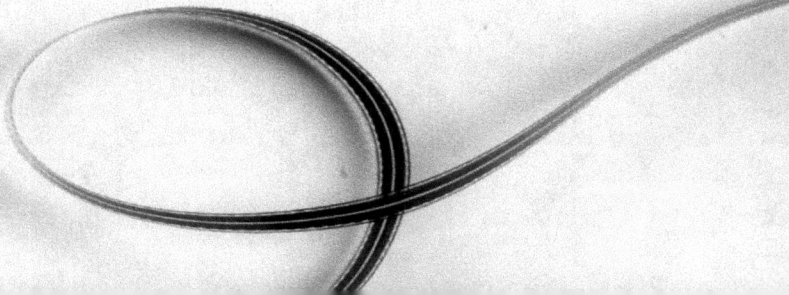

ROBERT REDFORD

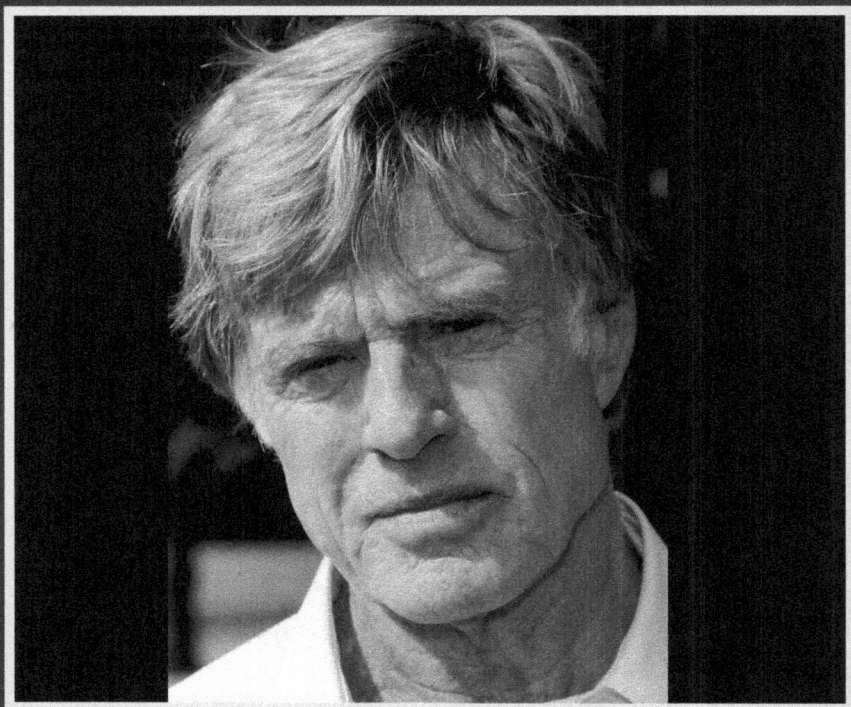

I WAS IN MY MID TWENTIES looking into the fashion world as a way to open another door, any door that would put me on a track, that might answer the question, "Why am I here?"

I was determined to stay in the States and found my next employer—the renowned men's fashion designer, Roland Meledandri. He had a stellar reputation for quality and his sophisticated shop on 56th Street in Manhattan was a gathering place for the art and entertainment world in the 60's and 70's.

When we met, Roland offered me a job that same day. He liked the way I sounded. He said I was ideal to play in the atmosphere he created, whatever that meant? So I accepted and soon found myself working with producers, actors and New York's elite. Interesting watching how men primped, of course they were peacocks, and a couple of rats.

Meledandri had a reputation for being very high-strung. He was known to break coat hangers in fits of rage. Our relationship had a great connection based on trust and after a short time he gave me permission to work the register, a big deal in the Meledandri world as he was preternaturally distrusting.

Ralph Lauren had worked for him and they began to form a partnership designing ties, but that failed when the label "Polo" was established and Ralph Lauren went on to become the legend he is today. I believe Roland was bitter. And that seed planted his inability to trust. Everyone eventually left.

One time, a regular customer came in to pick up a $3,000 suit and two days later he returned, seething. I was the one who gave him his final fitting, and when I questioned him about the alleged issue with the suit, the customer flew into a rage. I knew that no finished product ever left the premises short of perfection. That's what Roland demanded, and now in public his work and integrity were being questioned.

The customer stood in front of the mirror criticizing the tailoring. It

suddenly occurred to me that he went elsewhere, had it altered and came in ridiculing Roland in front of his customers. I whispered my assumption in Roland's ear. He just stared at me in shock that someone would do this.

I noticed that when the customer went to change, he had taken some shirts and a briefcase in with him. When he came out in a huff, I realized that he was also a thief as the merchandise was not in the dressing room. I took it upon myself to unlock his case when the customer wasn't looking. He argued with Roland about never coming back, and as he lifted his case to leave three shirts, a sweater fell out. Roland quietly told him to leave. The other customers were in shock, while the red-faced thief exited. I was embraced for finding the truth. God that felt good.

Robert Redford was a regular customer; his office was conveniently located above us. He would walk in with a cold attitude and ask if Roland was in. On three occasions my reply was "no, but . . ," and Redford would walk out without further response. I didn't find him to be the warmest individual but then again, who had no time for small talk?

After getting advice from Roland, I deployed a different tactic the next time Redford stepped halfway in.

Very quickly, I said, "Oh, Mr. Redford, a beautiful suit just came in and Mr. Meledandri INSISTS that you try it on."

He paused, gave me a questionable look, and then asked if anyone else was in the premises. I said "no" and then locked the door behind him, which he seemed to appreciate. Redford had great style and a terrific talent. He was just not an easy person to approach, and that was okay with me. It was a learning process.

I was twenty-six at the time and my head kept screaming, "Fuck, it's Robert Redford!" My family would not believe it. I appeared calm, keeping my excitement at bay. I pulled out a brown velvet suit with ivory buttons that made the icon smile. He tried on the jacket that complimented his fair complexion perfectly. As he stood in front of the mirror the usual routine was to slide your hands down the sides of the suit to give the feel of Meledandri's fine line. High-cut armpits and a button placed right on the stomach gave the client the illusion of being taller while cutting down on any protruding shape. That was his genius.

But as I touched the sides of Redford, I came across a pair of bar handles and swiftly said, "If you want to wear this, you must lose all this." I grabbed his excess. At that moment his mouth dropped open as did mine for my unbelievable audacity.

"Such a mouth," I thought.

He stared back at me, and after the initial shock dissipated he flashed that spectacular Redford smile and said, "You're absolutely right," and then broke into a laugh. He let me in. Goodie.

So Mister Redford, what looks good for supper?

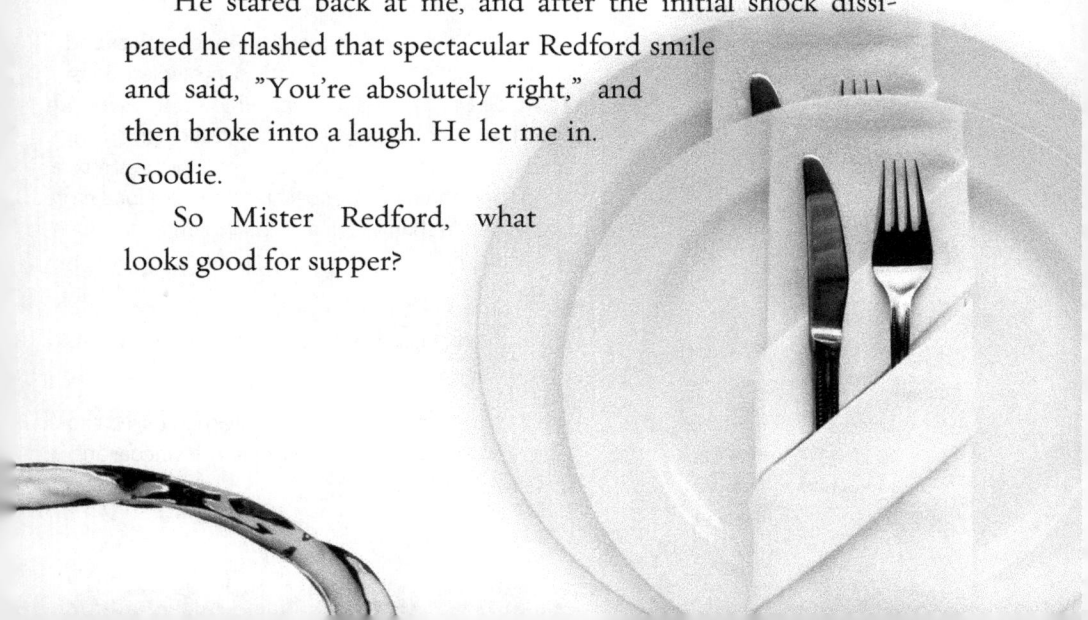

When I thought of Redford, I thought a little worldlier. He is a straight shooter, maybe not easily approached but I think would be faithful to those around him. He reminds me of someone whose appearance is never out of place. He is highly intelligent, elusive, present, tasteful and simple. He is down to earth, so I say why not "Paella?"

INGREDIENTS

3 tablespoon olive oil

1 tablespoon paprika

2 teaspoon dried oregano

1 1/2 pounds skinless and boneless chicken, cut into 2-inch pieces

salt and pepper to taste

4 cloves garlic (chopped finely)

1 teaspoon red-pepper flake

2 cups uncooked white rice

1 large pinch saffron

1 cup chopped Italian parsley

2 bay leafs

1 quart chicken stock

juice of 3 lemons

2 tablespoons olive oil

5 red tomatoes, sliced

1 chopped Spanish onion

1 coarsely chopped bell pepper

1 pound chorizo sausage, crumbled

1 pound shrimp (cleaned)

2 pounds Manila clams

1 pound squid (cleaned)

2 tablespoons olive oil

INSTRUCTIONS

In a bowl mix 3 tablespoons olive oil, oregano, paprika, salt and pepper. Stir in chicken pieces and cover.

In a large skillet, heat 3 tablespoons olive oil. Mix in garlic, red pepper flakes and rice. Cook for 5 minutes, then add bay leaf, parsley, saffron threads, chicken stock and lemon juice, finally adding sliced tomatoes. Simmer for 25 minutes.

Grill the sausages, when done slice ½-inches thick and set aside. Next in a pan, fry the squid in 3 tablespoons of olive oil. Drain excess oil on paper towel. In a separate skillet, heat 2 tablespoons olive oil and stir in the marinated chicken and onion and cook for 5 minutes. Mix in the sausage, tomatoes, pepper and tomatoes for 5 more minutes. Stir in shrimp, squid and clams until they open (10 minutes).

Spread out the rice mixture over the serving tray. Pour over all the other cooked ingredients and serve with lemon wedges.

With it I would serve a very finely shredded mixed cabbage salad and a dressing of olive oil, rice vinegar and soy sauce. Serves 4.

Australian opera singer Dame Nellie Melba performed in Paris in the late 1800's. A great chef named the peach and strawberry or (raspberry) dessert in her honor. It has been a Star ever since.

INGREDIENTS

4 cups of water

3 cups sugar

2 tablespoons lemon juice

1 vanilla pod, slit

6 peaches

strawberry sauce

3 cups strawberries

½ cup sugar

1 tablespoon lemon juice

1 large vanilla ice cream

1 cup whipped cream

INSTRUCTIONS

In a wide saucepan, add water, sugar, lemon juice and vanilla pod. When it begins to boil, simmer for a few minutes untill sugar dissolves.

Cut peaches in half and take out stones. Poach pears in sugar syrup for 5 minutes till soft. Spoon out and skin the peaches and set aside.

Liquidize strawberries, sugar and lemon juice in a blender.

Place a layer of whipped cream on the bottom of each cup, and ice cream on top. Pour over the strawberry syrup. Add the halved peach and repeat the process with the cream on top with a slice of peach. Add a waffle biscuit to each. Serves 6.

I remained a fan ever since, and happily for Roland and for me Redford bought the suit. Ten years later, at La Scale in Beverly Hills, I spotted him sitting with Paul Newman. What a sight, to see the two of them together. La Scale was no stranger to Hollywood wattage, but this pairing was the mother lode. As they were leaving, Redford stopped by my table to say hello. I could not believe he remembered. My friends from Australia who were having dinner with me slipped into shock. "You know Robert Redford?"

"Yes, I do but it's a long story."

They were impressed and I kept up my façade.

EILEEN DAVIDSON

HAD A CALL ONE morning from Executive Producer Ken Corday interested in reviving my character, Tony DiMera, on *Days of Our Lives*. An appointment was established to meet with him and the new head writer James Riley at the NBC studios. The last time I was there I had been asked up to the executive's office, the door automatically closed behind me as I faced expressions of doom. The fact is they are telling you that your services are no longer required and you try your best to act in a normal fashion. It can make an actor feel like they didn't make a

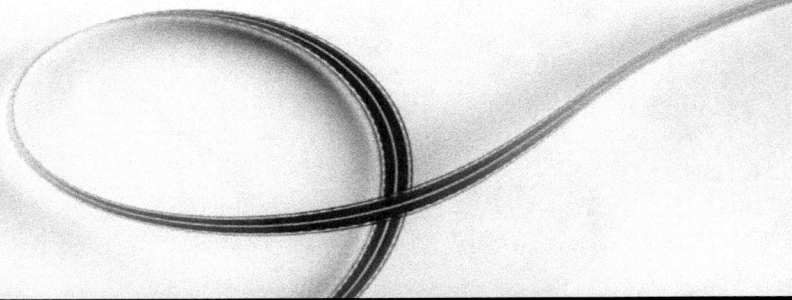

difference. In my mind's eye, I kept telling myself that fortune's heart was waiting elsewhere.

Five years later it was a new chapter and I was alive again in a world where death can revive itself by the miracle of a pen and the "Lazarus" effect is embraced. I entered the office where James Riley sat opposite the producer. I purposely dressed in a suit as the character was established as an aristocrat. Riley was meeting me for the first time and we hit it off. He had watched my series *Mission Impossible* and became curious. This was to be taken as a compliment as he was never interested in meeting actors only from a distance. To him they were puppets to play with. Riley also believed he would risk smashing the mystery that he had captured in his head about you. The meeting lasted for two hours with many laughs. I was being auditioned by a man who thought highly of his own sense of humor. All I kept thinking to myself was, "Do not get on the wrong side of this man because on the opposite end of that spectrum was a snake whose humor could turn deadly."

And the premonition that I had over the years turned out to be a true characteristic of James Riley. The tale of his origins revealed he was educated to be a Pediatrician but fainted when he witnessed his first birth. Because of his wicked humor in storytelling, he ended up putting his imaginative talents into writing soap operas. He was not a fan of older actors because he was more intrigued

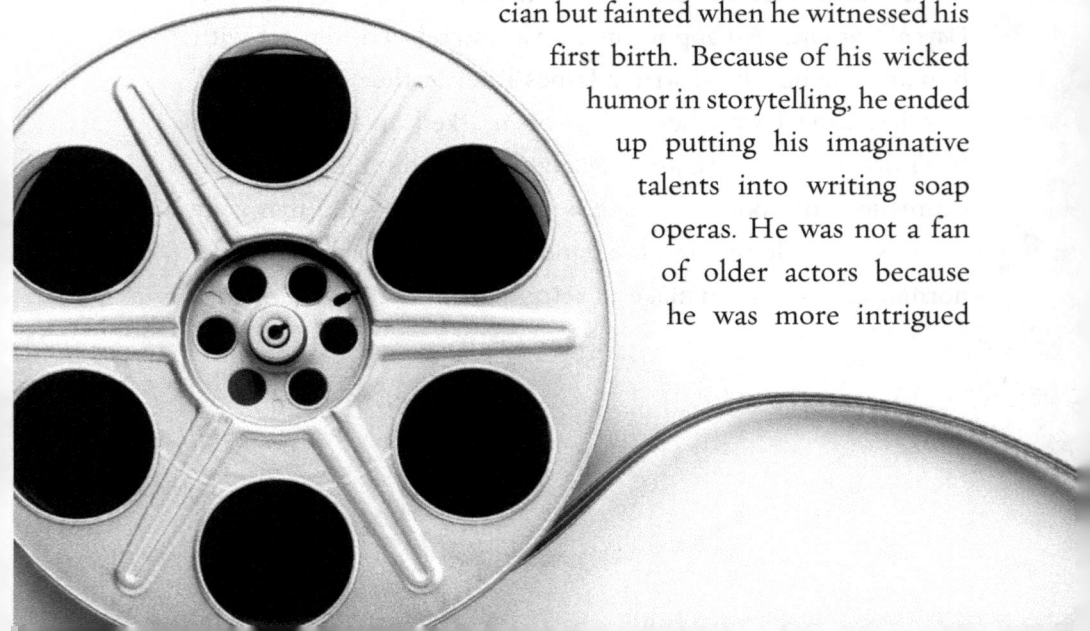

watching young sexy talent execute his imagination. Riley began to change the face of daytime with his over the top novellas at the expense of American family dramas. For a while it worked but in the end, like him, life became a cartoon.

I now had a new wife named "Kristen," who was played by the talented Eileen Davidson. It was then that the dynamics changed for my character in the show. She had betrayed me by having an affair with "John Black," the show's macho hero. We got off to a rocky start as I felt by her responses that I was imposing on her storyline of love in the afternoon. My character was now being written at effect rather than at cause and for the first time in my career the love scenes given became awkward and uncomfortable. She seemed to conduct the scene where I could and couldn't kiss her, because my darker make-up would infringe upon hers. So one day I started kissing her neck and then I drifted down to her breasts. I had to go somewhere to create the seduction. Somehow one breast popped out of her negligee exposing it on camera. The crew was delighted, she was furious. I did not blame her. I think she thought I did it on purpose. Maybe I did, but as a male I did not appreciate the lack of interest, after all it was just a show and not reality and we were being paid well for it. Things got bumpy after that.

I was asked to do an interview with *Soap Opera Digest* about what it was like to be back again in Daytime? "Wonderful," with my thoughts thinking, "Another trip to Egypt." When asked what the difference was working with my previous wife played by Leann Hunley compared to my present one with Eileen, I

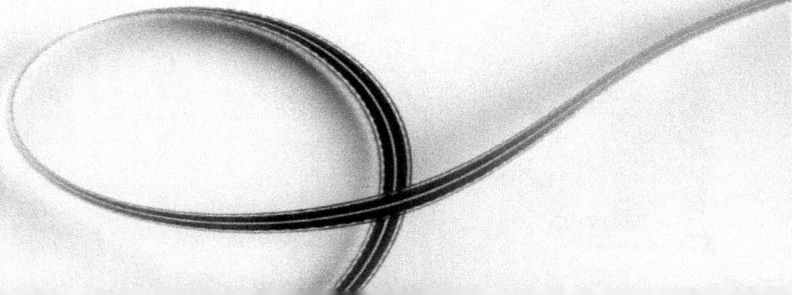

answered, "With Leann you could see her heart but with Eileen you have to find it."

That was not like me but I wanted to lash out. My parents had died a couple of months earlier and I felt raw. Again, I was outspoken and ended up paying a price. After it was published there was a loud knock on my dressing room door. When I said "Come in" Eileen flew through the door screaming and throwing books at me.

Somehow after that incident I was betrayed and my death on the show was again imminent. I had not had a chance to mourn my parent's transition and found my emotions being filtered through my performances. James Riley was informed that I disliked his writing, which was a lie, but he was ready for the kill. His humor had left him, which was what I suspected would eventually happen from the beginning. After that I settled into the relationship given.

Eileen was terrific and that year we both did some of our best work. Our conflict in the beginning had now disappeared. She looked beautiful and was always present. It was at this time the "Blindness" story was born, and my anticipation to be creative set in motion another finality. It didn't help that this particular story was voted one of the worst by *Soap Opera Digest*, the publication otherwise known as the "Bible of Daytime."

This probably irked Riley and whatever the reason for my next demise, James Reilly painted his canvas RED.

Death is no stranger to daytime television. If a storyline got tired, a death could liven things up. If an actor wasn't renewing a contract, death was a viable option for a swift and dramatic exit. If an actor was aging, unruly or simply deemed unnecessary to the plot, dying brought drama and closure. On and off the camera—not to mention in the hearts of devoted fans—death was a fever pitch of emotion. I wanted to leave quietly and just go off into the next stage of my life without regrets. Our team of players was doing complicated work in a business that was executed with breathtaking speed.

Before I had left the show, I had invited Eileen and her husband to my home for dinner as they were going to Greece for the first time. So as she was a vegetarian, I decided on "Yemista," stuffed vegetables, Greek style.

INGREDIENTS

4 red peppers

4 tomatoes

4 medium size squash

20 grape leaves

10 cabbage cups

1/3 cup olive oil

1 medium onion (chopped)

3 cloves garlic (minced)

salt and pepper

1 cup chopped parsley

½ cup chopped dill

½ cup chopped mint

1 cup pine nuts

½ cup raisins

2 cups long-grain rice

3 cups chicken broth

INSTRUCTIONS

Prepare by steaming cabbage shells (do not overcook) and fresh grape leaves (or bottled grape leaves, no steaming necessary) and put aside.

Cut the tops of peppers, squash and tomatoes and scoop out the pulp and discard. In a large pan, heat the oil and add the onions and garlic, salt, pepper, dill, mint, parsley and stir. Finally add pine nuts, raisins and rice. Stir all the ingredients together for a few minutes. Fill the vegetables with the ingredients but only half way to give room for the expansion of the rice, raisins and pine nuts, and place the lids back on top. Spoon in one tablespoon of mixture into the cabbage cups and roll together. Repeat the same with the grape leaves.

In a large saucepan, place the cabbage and grape leave rolls on the bottom, then the squash, peppers and tomatoes on top. Add the chicken broth, cover and cook for 30 minutes until rice is done. Serves 4.

Next, how to prepare the Tzatziki…

INGREDIENTS

1 long cucumber, seeded and grated

1 teaspoon salt

15 ounces Greek yogurt

2 cloves garlic (minced)

1 ounce ouzo

2 tablespoons chopped fresh dill

1 tablespoon red wine vinegar

2 tablespoons olive oil

INSTRUCTIONS

In a large bowl, stir together all the ingredients and add olive oil until all ingredients are thoroughly combined.

When the multitude of stuffed vegetables are done place on individual plates and serve hot with Tzatziki on the side. Serves 4.

Served with Vanilla Cream

INGREDIENTS

2 cups all-purpose flour

2 teaspoons baking soda

½ teaspoon ground cloves

1 teaspoon ground cinnamon

½ cup unsweetened coconut

½ teaspoon salt

1½ cups sugar

4 eggs

1/3 cup chopped walnuts

1/3 cup chopped macadamia nuts

¾ cup vegetable oil

2 cups ripe mango (cut into small cubes

CREAM

1 cup heavy cream

2 tablespoons sugar

1 teaspoon vanilla

INSTRUCTIONS

Pre-heat oven to 350° F. Grease with butter a 9 x 6 loaf pan. In a bowl, combine the flour, coconut, baking soda, cinnamon, cloves and salt. Add the sugar, eggs, nuts and oil. Add mango and slowly fold into the flour mixture. Pour ingredients into the greased pan and bake for 45 minutes. Test to see if cooked by placing knife in center and that it comes out clean.

CREAM

Add sugar and vanilla to the cream and whip up until cream is stiff. Serve on top of sliced mango cake.

GREEK COFFEE

For each demitasse cup, add one measured cup of water, one heaped teaspoon of Greek coffee, half-teaspoon sugar and a pinch of cardamom into a Greek pot. Keep stirring until the coffee begins to rise and turn off. Pour into cups and serve with dessert.

I did dodge bullets staying alive in this very competitive game. Eileen proved to be a no-nonsense lady and a great actress to work with, even with those challenges in the beginning I loved it and grew as an actor because of it. Last year she won her first Emmy as Best Actress and Eileen is now working on the reality series Beverly Hills Housewives.

JENNIFER AND
JOHN ANISTONN

I FIRST MET JENNIFER ANISTON celebrating success at NBC's annual gathering of stars at its studio in Burbank, California. It was in the late spring of 1995 when John Aniston who I had worked with for many years on *Days of Our Lives* introduced me to his lovely daughter. Very sexy with that down-to-earth voice, her manner without airs, she was now living and succeeding in NBC's big hit *Friends*. What we had in common, which I did not know at the time, was the passing of my friend and her godfather Telly Savalas. He died in 1994, and the wonderful service

took place at the Greek Orthodox Cathedral of St. Sophia in 1971. I didn't know the Aniston's at the time, but heard they were there also paying their respects. As a matter of fact when Jennifer was starring in her movie *The Break-up*, as a homage to her Godfather, she looked in the mirror and said to herself, "Who loves ya baby?" quoting Savalas's iconic line.

John and Telly were great mates; in fact the *Kojak* star was also best man at his first marriage.

"We were friends since high school. He was unique, one of a kind, his only flaw was he could never say "No" especially to family." But it was John's mother Stella Anastasakis who was the greatest influence on Jennifer. Her grandmother frequented the Greek Orthodox Church of St. George in Media, Pennsylvania, and like her granddaughter, a very classy lady who was always also well dressed. Stella had very strong ties to the church and when she passed away in the 1990's, Jennifer donated a large sum of money to the congregation in memory of her beloved grandmother. One thing that surprised me about John was he wanted to be a doctor in Greece and so he left a five-year old Jennifer behind with her grandmother.

"So how would you say she turned out?" I asked.

"Very sweet, down to earth, a good business woman, generous, pretty good," he said with a faint smile. One thing about John, his descriptions are short and to the point.

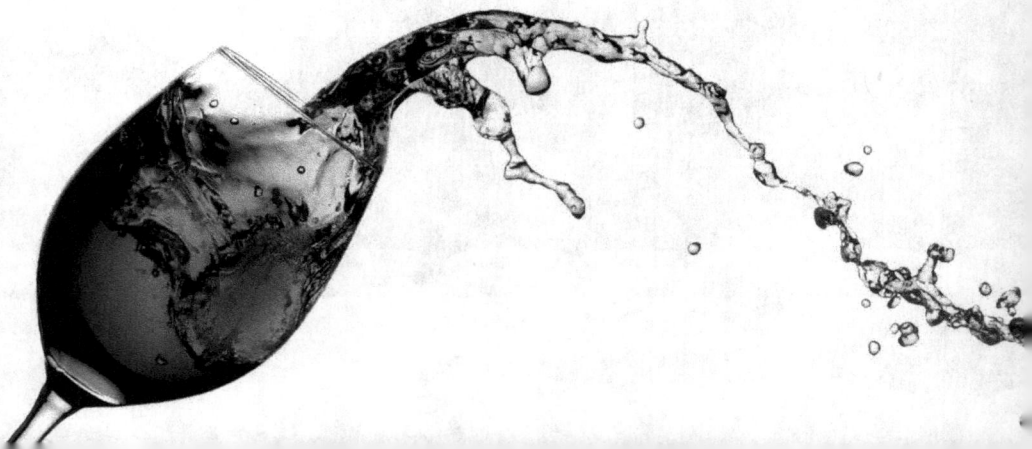

I must say he was always a pleasure to work with, a pro who never carried any drama onto a set, no ego, just real and I think Jennifer inherited some of his lack of pretension. I enjoyed speaking Greek to John when it was necessary to exchange a private moment on the set. And on a rare occasion, we would talk about Jennifer and Brad Pitt when he was his son-in-law. John was never about gossip, and if that was your interest he would simply move on. In the exchanges I had with Jennifer, she seemed to love her privacy as well. Maybe that was part of their Greek heritage too, never to bring shame on the family that is very deeply rooted in our ancestry. In short, "None of your bloody business," or simply not everyone is entitled to your truth.

In early spring of 2015, I met with John at a café close to NBC Studios. There, two Greek-American guys sat, one born in Crete and the other from Australia, catching up over sips of Virgin Mary's. We reflected about the nasty consequences we experienced on *Days of Our Lives* when we survived the vengeance of head writer James Riley. My punishment was three over-the-top deaths conducted by his Lordship while John was placed in a coma for a year and a half. John supposedly had said after being asked by a journalist, "How is your new storyline?" Aniston responded, "Boring."

James Riley's wrath after he heard tales that did not applaud him, his form of "Death by Head Writer" was the weapon

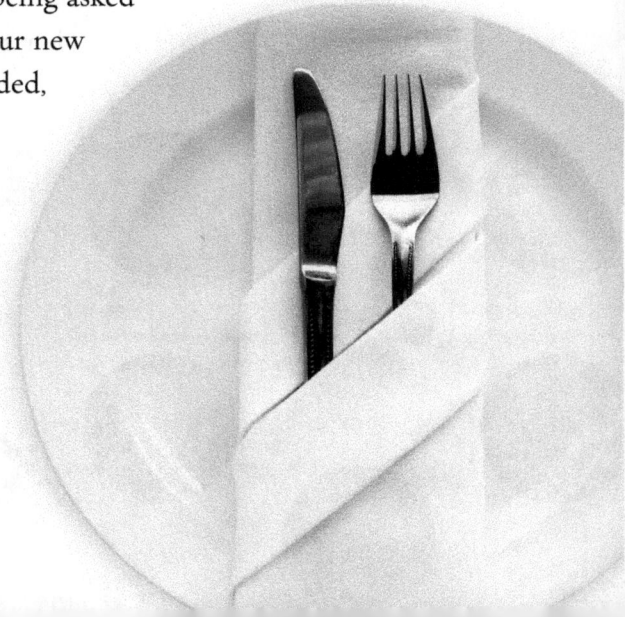

used just to remind the thespian who was conducting. We both had a good laugh in retrospect. We really loved *Days*: it was our second home. A few years ago sadly the poor man Reilly died from an overdose of ice cream.

Speaking of food "What is Jennifer's favorite?"

"Mexican, she doesn't like lamb," John replied with a chuckle. "A Greek and she doesn't like Lamb?" I sounded surprised.

But then that seemed to relate to her earthy-tone personality. I felt without asking that she would be very comfortable in men's company. I think she is also very seductive. The closest I got to be with her in *Friends* was when they used a clip of me out of *Days of Our Lives* for one of their segments. I've been getting residuals ever since. How to appear without appearing?

We both agreed we loved all type of cuisines, even our own. Our mothers loved to over-cook. But that was a different era. These days most things are eaten almost raw. I like a bit of both. John is about simplicity. When he spoke of his daughter, there was no ego or pride in his tone, his feelings private. I suddenly recalled what economy John has in his demonstrations of life when speaking. Quiet and intimate he converses only with a sense of privacy. We both came from old school traditions where formality reigned. That too has a way of sustaining memory and how it expresses itself through the physical. Of course, deeply and privately he has enormous admiration and love for his treasure.

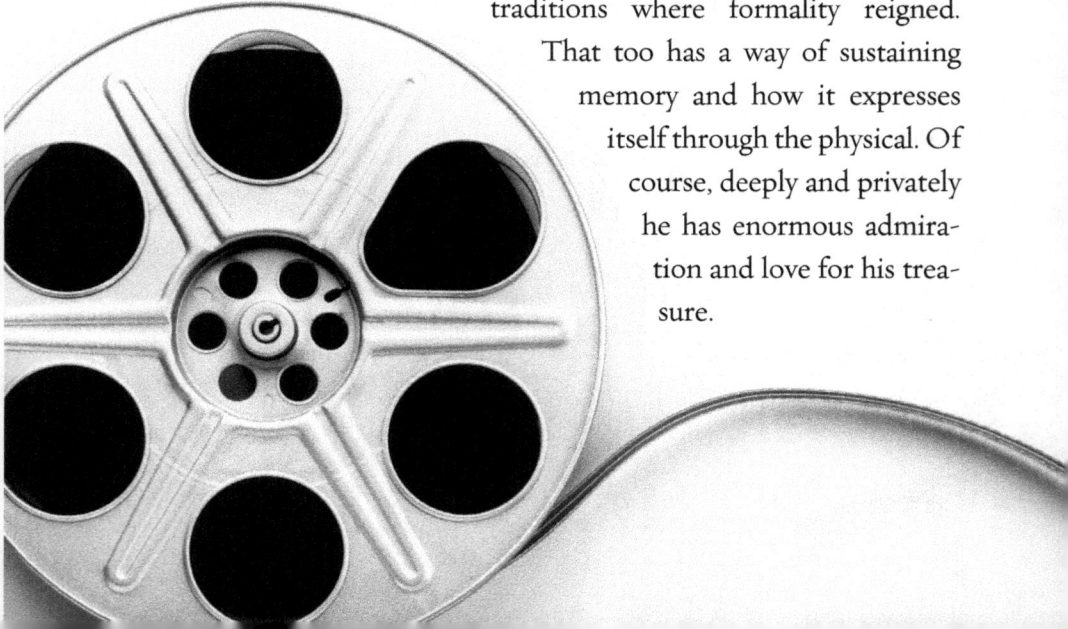

At the end of that morning, we spoke of how, even though we have lived well in this business, we agreed that we would never recommend this life to any young person with what we know now. You have to keep waking up and dreaming of this business to sustain yourself throughout. That kind of perseverance was for a special kind of warrior, who understood that when you fall down you fall forward. That way when you get up you're ahead.

As we left each other with Greek hugs without apology, we parted just as we met, quietly. He has had a good life but not without its struggles. He is still smiling in his later years and still working when few at his age have retired without a choice. Jennifer's life continues to shine brightly. She is at the top of her game and as an icon to many women trying to emulate her. The life continues.

So I decided what would satisfy my Greek friends for their evening's taste buds? I thought "Think heart, think earth, a cuisine that you would share over a no-show business conversation over?" So here it is.

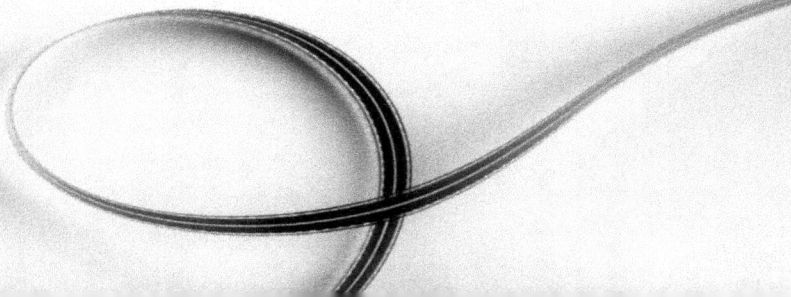

*I never knew a Greek that didn't love seafood. After all, didn't
Greek gods emerge from the ocean? So let's indulge . . .*

INGREDIENTS

2 pounds mussels

2 pound little neck clams

1 tablespoon tomato paste

5 ripe tomatoes, peeled and
puréed

5 tablespoons olive oil

5 tablespoonschopped parsley

3 cloves garlic (finely chopped)

4 tablespoons basil, finely
chopped

1 small dried red chile

1 teaspoon shredded ginger

1 flat teaspoon sugar

1 tablespoon balsamic vinegar

salt and pepper

INSTRUCTIONS

Scrub the mussels and the clams. Discard any that won't
close. In a large pot, add 1 cup of water with mussels and
clams. Cover and bring to boil.

Turn off and let the shellfish steam and open. Mix tomato
paste with 2 tablespoons water and pour into the puréed
tomatoes. Heat oil in a large pan and add the garlic, cooking liquid and tomato paste, herbs, ginger chile, sugar
and vinegar.

Season with salt and pepper and simmer for 30 minutes.
Take the mussels and clams and add them to the mixture
with or without shells. Serve with toasted garlic bread.
Serves 4.

INGREDIENTS

3 cups penne pasta

3 tablespoons melted butter

1½ cups Parmesan cheese

1½ pounds ground beef

¾ cup dry white wine

1 large red onion (chopped)

2 garlic cloves (finely chopped)

1 can tomato sauce (large)

½ teaspoon cinnamon

½ teaspoon Allspice

salt to taste

1½ cups Parmesan cheese

INSTRUCTIONS

Heat the oil in a large sauté pan. Add ground beef and cook until pink disappears. Add sautéd onions into meat and stir through. Add tomato sauce, wine, garlic, Allspice, cinnamon, salt and pepper and let it simmer for 15 minutes. Cook the pasta noodles, drain and set aside.

Into pasta pot melt ½ cup melted butter and return the cooked noodles to the pot. Stir in one cup grated cheese and toss lightly.

Brush a large pan with olive oil. Lay down approximately half the pasta noodles until flat. Add meat and spread on even layered over the pasta. And then top again with the remaining noodles.

Béchamel Sauce (see Jackie Kennedy recipe of Moussaka w/Béchamel).

Pour over the Béchamel Sauce into every corner and finally sprinkle the rest of the cheese on top.

Bake in 350° F. oven for approximately 50 minutes or until golden brown. Yields 12 servings.

Serve over an Arugula Salad with vinaigrette dressing.

This is a traditional Kastellorizian, Greek dessert that all our grandmothers made. So in memory of John's mother and Jennifer's beloved grandmother, I present my family's special dessert.

INGREDIENTS

2½ cups plain flour

pinch salt

1 cup warm water

1 teaspoon olive oil

1 pound butter

large pan

1½ cups sugar

1 tablespoon ground cloves

1 tablespoon Cinnamon

INSTRUCTIONS

Sift flour into a large bowl. Make a well in the middle and add salt, oil and some water. Mix enough water to make soft dough, and then start to knead. Keep working the dough to get the consistency. It should be a little sticky.

Put aside for no less than 1/2-hour and then sprinkle work surface with flour. Melt half the butter while rolling out dough and then stretch from center out. When rolled out thinly into a large circular shape, pour on butter and coat all over the dough. Use hands to spread.

Make a hole in the middle of the circle and fold out making the hole larger. Also roll out the edges. Keep folding until you have a long strip (snake like). Squeeze the long snake shape and then twist like a skipping rope, twirling the dough. Take one end and make a little hole and then spiral the dough around this. Do the same to the other end, and then lay one spiral on top of the other. Before cooking, place this in fridge for about 10 minutes to cool to make it easier to roll (no sticking). Remove from fridge and roll out quite thin. (To fit pan)

Sprinkle with water before frying. Fry on low heat in melted butter (2 ounces or more as needed) till brown. Turn over. (Add more butter if needed)

Once cooked use a fork or hands (very hot, wear gloves) and pull the pastry apart into thin strips and pieces. Add sugar and ground cloves and toss through hot pastry. Use as much as is needed to get required taste. Serves 4.

I always loved this dessert. I like the texture, spiciness and its sweet taste. And you know what, it's also because I remembered my grandmother Polexeni making it. Giving you something to eat somehow becomes more tasteful when there is a grandmother behind it.

It was a nice feeling spending the morning with an old friend. Even though it had been quite a few years since seeing each other, there was no adjustment to be made. Dinner would have been a delight for all three of us, we these three generations.

Three weeks after John and I parted, a message from Corday productions came welcoming me back to the family of *Days*. Unexpected and appreciated, my life as a long distance runner was not over.

THE LAST OF THE M.I.
TEAM—LIVING THE DREAM

WE NUMBERED FIVE WHEN the *Mission Impossible* team began in 1988 on the Gold Coast of Australia's Northern Shores. It was an exciting time for all of us to continue where the old iconic team of the 70's left off and only Peter Graves of the original program had been asked back.

The arrival of one of the longest strikes in Writer's Guild history was alive and well shutting the industry down in Hollywood, hence the transporting of *Mission Impossible* to Australia outside of the Guild's jurisdiction. We had to fit the old dialogue and attitudes from the 70's into the late 80's. The writing was forbidden to change until the strike broke months later. At

that time we were into our fifth script when changes to the face of the original series began to breathe a new life.

The great production team from the U.S. and Australia came together quickly and *Mission Impossible*, the revival was born. It was a new frontier in this tropical environment. We had baptized the new Dino De Laurentis studio, which was later bought out and converted to the Warner Bros sister company, "Village Roadshow." It existed in the middle of the bush where a few miles away a beautiful 100-mile stretch of beach provided sanctuary. You could easily get lost in a place where little culture thrived and drinking at the bar was the main form of entertainment with the occasional drunken bravado. But we worked six days a week and there was little time to play. The one good thing that I had never experienced before was going home to Australia after an emotional exit where many thought I was living a fantasy of making it in America. I was now in a world-recognized series where my family could celebrate my new success against those faulty soothsayers. Vengeance won out and I truly loved my work in the series with my newfound family especially Phil Morris and Jane Badler, who have remained true friends after all these years. We were all living the dream.

One wake-up experience took place on an early Monday morning when I drove to Broad beach, my favorite swimming hole before going to the studio. After riding and crashing into

those frothy waves against the sunrise, I always felt exhilarated. Now ready to face my day's challenges and all the wonderful new technology I would play with as a spy, I returned to my car. To my surprise four hostile plain-clothes policemen were standing by my rented automobile, when the senior police officer in an accusatory manner demanded, "Open your fucking trunk."

Confused with the attitude and tone, I did as he requested. When one of his fellow officers blurted out, "Don't you know who he is?"

"I don't give a fuck," was his response.

While they were searching the rest of my car I asked what they were looking for? Drugs I thought.

"You think you can come to our country and break our laws, well you can't."

Slightly confused and trying to find some humanness in all of this I responded,

"But I was born here officer just like you, I was only out for a swim."

"Well we don't want you here, we're not good enough? Go back to America where you belong," he said pointedly.

They obviously had very little respect for artists. Their racism was shining through. Not finding anything illegal, they stormed off, leaving the trunk and all four doors left wide open.

Talk about dumping their hostility on what was an innocent and beautiful experience. Disturbed by that unexplainable behavior, I reported it to my producers who warned us all that the cops were giving tickets to any kind of violation because they thought our industry "too arrogant" and wanted it brought down to size. That tall poppy syndrome of, "If they get too tall shoot them down," I had grown up with was alive and well. In weeks to come the crew got many tickets for DUI's or speeding while the actors remained untouched. Otherwise we loved the beauty, generosity and friendliness of the people in this world of tropical Australia.

That unnecessary experience was rare, it was good to be home in the state where my father in his youth migrated from Greece and began working in the cane fields of the tropical north. And now his eldest son was back in that state where it all started, going beyond his father's early struggles and rewarding him for his investment and hard labor.

In my training, it was always important as an actor to make sure my body and spirit were kept lucid, healthy and not living in excess, to deal with the demands of a grueling six-day shoot. I used to love rewarding myself on my one day off with a massage, to get all the built-up tension released and use that recuperating time going within, through meditation. It was a wonderful combination that I continue with today.

When I had to fit into a new mask, I was called in at 3:30 a.m. for all the different applications to resolve the complexities of the next character I was to impersonate. It was a tiring and claustrophobic process that took hours and then breathing

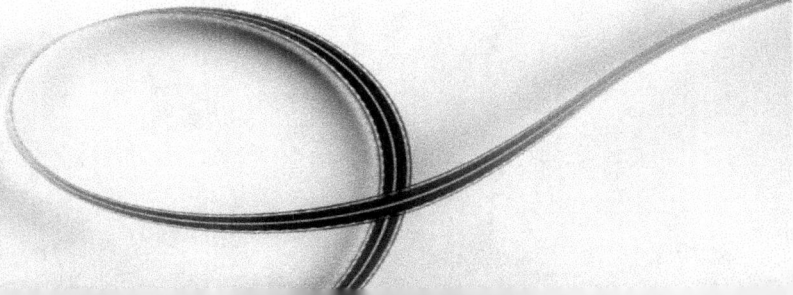

Jane Badler flirting (as usual) with our head grip, Tony.

through a straw until they were ready for me to unmask. It was an ordeal and took time getting use to it. Each mask cost $5,000, and I could not afford to screw it up. In Queensland we were going through birthing pains, which was expected. Still we pulled it off and our team of creators was the best especially the production designers.

One day feeling exhausted, my hairdresser for the show recommended a great masseur that she had been intimate with called Tom. He really excelled in his work and the gentle giant was a well-built 32-year-old athlete. I had made a new friend in

this isolating environment where sometimes the fine line of fan and friendship could bleed over.

Occasionally after a session, we would break bread at one of the many wonderful restaurants or take a walk along the beach, exchanging stories of our life's experiences. One such evening when the waves were crashing wildly onto the shore, the wind howling and whistling through the apartment corridors setting off a dramatic but ominous environment, my new friend Tom paused suddenly. He was staring up at a large window on the corner of a small apartment building. As he stopped the shadow of a figure was seen crossing behind the drawn curtain. I asked, "What's so interesting about that apartment? Do you have another client up there?"

Without even looking in my direction, he simply stated without emotion, "No but I was up there last night represent-ing another client who was owed money, and when I asked this person to finalize his debt, he refused. And so I had no choice but to break his legs. That's what I do on the side, break things, fingers, depending on how far I have to go to satisfy my client . . . . Does that change things between us my friend?"

I froze. Then he looked at me calmly but deadly. Shocked with this unexpected revelation, I said, "Have you ever killed anyone?"

He continued to walk into the howling wind without answering. There was nothing left to say, picture complete, the mystery had been revealed. I will never forget that face whose

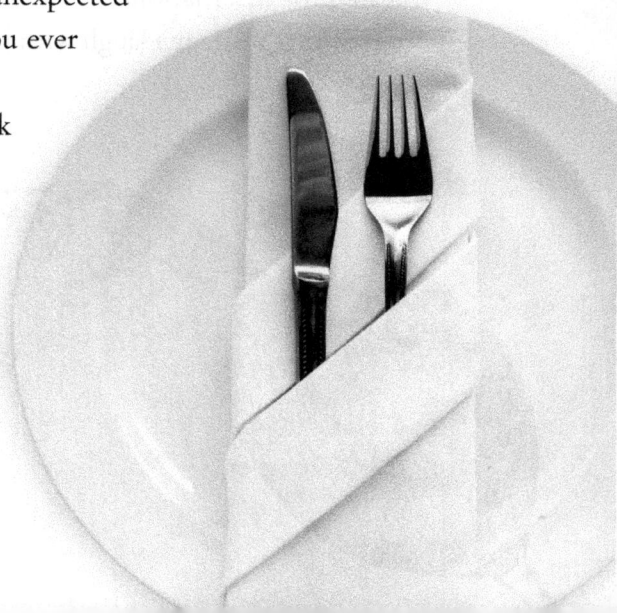

mask had just dropped off out of nowhere. On television I was playing "Nicholas Black" whose expertise were masks and disguises. But this was real. I felt I was in the middle of a *Mission Impossible* episode without the team coming to my rescue. It made me feel dirty and creepy. I never mentioned this saga to anyone until I revealed it to Phil recently. He was stunned.

"Oh man, what happened next?"

I never saw him again, nor did he ever try to reach me. That warning was a wake-up call, to not always let my guard down until I am completely sure of the masked soul that crosses my path. Thank God I survived that, although I felt unclean having allowed that criminal to enter my personal and vulnerable space. Massages were put on the back burner for a long time.

In the second year, we moved down to Melbourne where the culture was immense. Jane Badler met her future husband, the wonderful Steven Hains and decided to settle in Australia after the series was over. Again *MI* became a success by finding the many suitable establishments that duplicated the international flavor of the show. Every week our destiny took us to another exotic local. As a Greek journalist said to me in Athens while being interviewed for the series, "Thaao, my Greek friend you are now International."

It always made me laugh with that heavy accent.

Jane and Peter on set in Melbourne.

I must say the food was always fresh and the seafood the best I had ever tasted. Since I had left years ago, Australia now had an international cuisine because of those varied immigrants who brought their culture along and gave OZ its diversity of unique flavors. We always believed that food was the great reward given our hard work and for surviving this tough business. It was the best nourishment to self. And it rewarded you back by the way you responded.

We only did 37 episodes but it was a series we were all proud of. I will always love the character of "Nicholas Black," the master of disguise. The name was given to me over dinner while breaking bread

Some of the many faces of "Nicholas Black."

with the executive producers before going to Australia. One asked, "What would you like to be called?"

"Well I always liked the name "'Nicholas,'" I said.

"Good" he responded, "And you're dark, so let's go with "'Nicholas Black.'"

And that's how that name was born, simply.

Every one of us had their place within the team and the players executed their parts well except for Tony Hamilton who seemed to be somewhere else. Jane was the femme fatale seductive and delicious, while Phil Morris played his kick-ass role as well as our technology expert with great panache.

We all eventually went back to the U.S. except for Jane Badler. She married well and had two sons along the way. Jane would always keep in touch as we all did with each other throughout the years. Anthony Hamilton who represented the muscle of the series died tragically at an early age. He was graced with much beauty but was lost as a human being. Adopted at the age of two from England by an Australian military family from Adelaide, he never had a clue where his true identity lay.

Phil Morris in Melbourne with the "Natives."

So when I saw him last the sadness that lay deeply within that conflicted personality never saw the light. He had died of AIDS at age of 42. That was a sad time for all of us.

Peter Graves died from a heart attack at the age of 84, always the gentleman who moved with the grace of the tennis player he was. That twinkle in the eye that set him apart from other players remained an enigma right up to his passing. I loved his face that looked like a roadmap of life's experiences. A true pro and a no-nonsense player, he was loved by all.

It's been 24 years since we all parted, but somehow the last of the team still celebrates the birth of our coming together with great food and wine. So recently in the spring of 2015 as we did on many other occasions, met at my home in the Hollywood hills. We talked about many things including Jane's new album as her wonderful singing had taken off internationally while Phil had just completed another series with always many other things brewing. They were simply great people, and I realized how blessed we all were that in this transient business something about our connection still resonated today. Phil is a powerful looking figure, a student of Wing Chun Kung Fu; he is a beautiful soul where for many years we spent hours upon hours exchanging our views on becoming.

We talked about how we all got our individual roles with Phil taking over where his father finished off, which did not come easily as he had to earn that right through the auditioning process, while Jane was brought in to replace the former player Terry Markwell late in the first season. My getting the part is already discussed in the chapter with Anthony La Paglia. We recalled when discussing our characters with the producers, their advice when questioned about motive was, "Don't think about it. Your characters are so smart they know what they are doing."

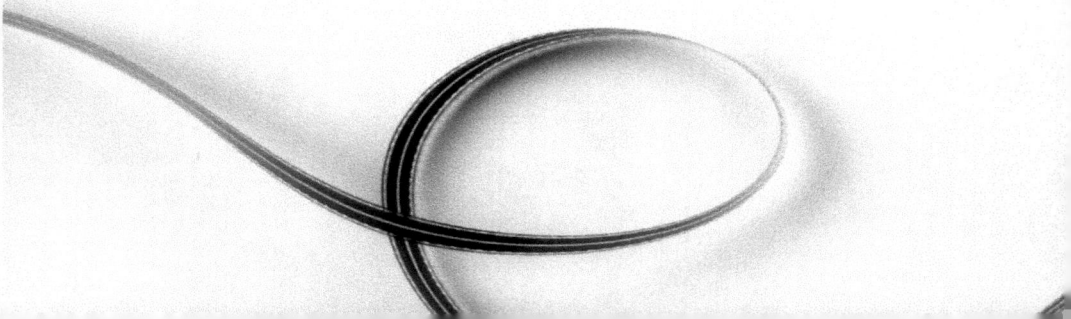

It came across like a blank. We had been chosen for the parts and like everyone else including the writers: it was a work in progress.

Phil mentioned that his father was not excited with the idea of a re-make, and never believed his son would get the part. It seemed like that with many of us, he had to prove his station and that he did well. I remembered how Peter was not so easily accessible early on until I broke his façade, when shooting an opening sequence; I faced him dead on and said, "Do you mind listening?"

I felt he was on rote and he thought his presence was enough. Peter certainly made a point of listening after that and we were fine. Phil recalled something I told him when shooting a sequence in Melbourne during a troubled time, "Take a chance, even when you fall, you still have moved forward after you've gotten up."

Jane mentioned that when she was called in, the network was very hush-hush about it; it was all done in secret. That's why we were all upset when she replaced Terry Markwell; our team had been broken up. But she surprised us with her love affair with Australia. That's why she stayed in OZ to find what she believed would be the true love of her life, and that she did when she discovered Steven Hains. With her wonderful singing talent she added

it to her character of "Shannon Reid" and seduced whoever crossed her path. Jane was a wonderful flirt, a free spirit that left her crew flirting back. She just oozes sex, without any effort. That's why we all loved our Jane. She always made us feel loved and appreciated.

With Heirloom Tomatoes

INGREDIENTS

16 small heirloom tomatoes

16 thin slices, Spanish prosciutto

4 balls of burrata

1 bunch basil

black pepper

olive oil

balsamic vinegar

INSTRUCTIONS

Wrap burrata (a semi-soft cheese made from Mozzarella and cream) in Spanish prosciutto and place in individual bowls.

Add 4 chopped tomatoes in each and sprinkle with finely sliced basil. Add olive oil and balsamic vinegar on top.

Add cracked black pepper. Serve with toasted garlic crostini. Serves 4.

With Basmati Rice

INGREDIENTS

1 large red snapper fillet
20 medium shrimp (shelled and cleaned)
12 scallops
2 dozen manila clams
olive oil
flour for coating

CURRY SAUCE

2 sticks butter
1 large chopped onion
2 cloves garlic
4 tablespoons madras curry powder
1 teaspoon turmeric
½ teaspoon cloves
½ teaspoon cinnamon
1 sliced banana
½ cup shredded coconut
4 ounces raspberry Jam
2 tablespoons honey
1 cup chicken broth
2 kafir leaves
parsley
mango chutney

INSTRUCTIONS

Cut the flour-coated fish fillets into 2-inch strips and fry in olive oil and put aside. Steam shrimp and drain. Pan fry flour-coated scallops until golden brown on both sides and mix delicately into shrimp and fish.

Steam clams until opened and remove from shells and place with other seafood and put clam juice aside.

CURRY SAUCE

In a deep pan, melt 1 stick of butter and add onion and garlic. When done, add all the spices together stirring constantly for 2 minutes. Add chopped banana, coconut, jam, kafir leaves and keep stirring.

Pour in chicken and 1-cup clam broth to mixture. Remove kafir leaves and gently add all the seafood and chopped parsley together. Serve hot over steamed Basmati rice and mango chutney. Serves 4.

This is a dessert I enjoyed in Havana prepared by my friend Rafaela.

INGREDIENTS

4 whole eggs

4 egg yolks

2 cups milk

1/3 cup water

1 ½ cups sugar

1 teaspoon vanilla essence

1 lemon peel

1 cinnamon stick

whipped cream

whole vanilla beans

INSTRUCTIONS

To prepare the caramel: In a small saucepan, add ¾ cups of sugar into the water and cook until the sugar begins to melt, constantly stirring until the sugar begins to caramelize. Remove from the heat and pour into muffin pan, covering the bottom and sides of the each compartment in the pan.

Next, place the milk, cinnamon stick and lemon peel into a saucepan and bring to a boil (medium heat). Stir the milk constantly when it begins to scald. Remove from stove and let it cool for 20 minutes. Remove the cinnamon and lemon peel.

Beat the eggs and egg yolks and vanilla and remaining sugar in a large bowl. Pour the milk into the bowl and then strain the bowl ingredients into the each compartment of the muffin pan covered with the caramel coating.

Put the muffin tray inside a large pan filled with 1-inch of water. Bake at 350° F. for approximately 1 hour. Insert a knife in the center of one serving to make sure it comes out dry.

Remove from oven and let cool. Insert knife around edges to loosen flan, and then cover muffin pan with the serving tray and turn upside down until flan falls. Serve warm or cold with whipped cream and dark chocolate, and garnish with vanilla beans. Serves 4.

FINDING THE
SEED INSIDE HAVANA

Havana at dawn.

WITH SWEEPING CHANGES IN U.S. relations with Cuba, the elusive island is now fair game for American tourism with no special favors or requisites. Well, sort of. Previously, only religious, cultural and educational groups could travel to Castro's domain, and with special permission from the State Department at that. Now, Americans can travel to Cuba without meeting the previous predicates so long as the trip is under the umbrella of a Cuba travel organization baring an official license from the U.S. State Department.

It's a curious and complex country, one worth visiting soon if you are an intrepid traveler and long to experience a taste of Cuba before the next round of tourism begins shifting things.

The first time I traveled to Havana it was more of a spiritual mission, visiting churches in pursuit of experiencing "faith" in a communist country known for cigars and repression; a place where God was usurped by dictatorship. I was hell bent on excavating Cuba's religious core, to see where hope and prayer slept, not to mention the unexpected.

Most churches in Havana are Roman Catholic, filled with statues of martyrs. There was a lot of sadness in those churches. Not much revelation. I was especially intrigued by the Santeria religion. Its roots stemmed from Nigeria, transported to the Caribbean by the Lucumi people in the late 18th century.

During my brief stay there, I orchestrated a session with a Babalao, a priest whose religion studies nature and the universe. Their primary function is to assist people in finding, understanding and being in alignment with one's individual destiny. Sounded good to me. I had been transported by car to the outskirts of Havana where the police (secret or in uniform) were always visible, even stopping or following us by car.

Sometimes you have to embrace blind faith, take risks and just go for it. I didn't know what to expect, though I suspected the experience would be otherworldly, or old worldly. In the end, it was both. In a private backyard surrounded by an abundance of plants, all sacred to the rituals, I was stripped and cleansed with herbs in front of a "shrine of worship." The shrine was overflowing with

deities. Apparently, this was considered a sacred space with a "born again" objective. It was overwhelmingly sensory, so much so that I was aroused. It didn't seem to embarrass them as much as it did me. I tried to forget about my nakedness and aroused state and just tried to be in the moment of whatever was happening there. I started getting into the trippy nature of it all— until a chicken was sacrificed as part of the closing ceremony. It was shocking and stunning, and I had to face away from the deities when the animal made its transition. It was harsh. And it wasn't yet over.

At the final stage of the ceremony, I was instructed to turn around as the priest dropped three open coconuts at my feet. How they fell would reveal the

outcome and intent of this secret ceremony. All three turned up white and were touching one another.

The priest smiled and said, "It is a good omen, when the spirits have sent you kisses." A strange euphoria eventually set in, which apparently signaled that the cleansing was successful.

That trip I also spent time in Havana with artists I met along the way. The simplicity in the way they lived, surrounded by poverty, their passion and love flowing freely offered a stark perspective to what I see and experience back home. I sat with these artists and while sharing an entire bottle of vodka they told tales of Castro's Cuba and I told tales of life in Hollywood. I gifted my host a watch as a gesture of thanks. His guests were amazed at my generosity and frankly I thought nothing of it. It was a gesture of appreciation—and ultimately a betrayal of my ignorance that a gift to a new friend in Cuba could cause havoc. Police would soon be stopping him on the street. Curious about the quality of his watch, and where he would have obtained such a fine piece of jewelry, they would accuse him of stealing and smashed his wrist against the wall. He would let out a loud cry and they would arrest him. He was eventually discharged. All this commotion took place because he had been given a gift he himself could not afford.

Despite the roadblocks of that first trip to Cuba, I was eager to return to Havana when the travel siren once again called my

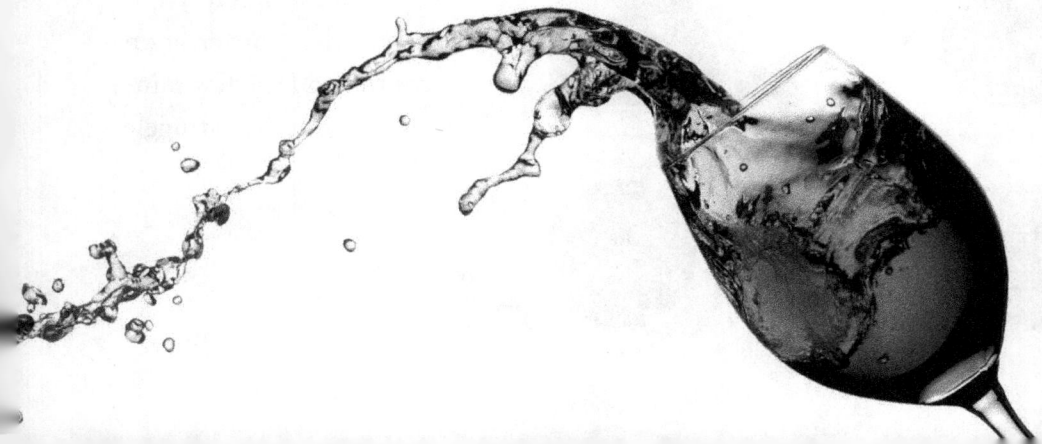

ISIS and other factors steered me away from the region and I found myself Miami bound.

Havana was under a great deal of construction this time, finally restoring much of the city's great architecture. I visited a number of its landmarks including the Museum of the Revolution, the Napoleonic Museum and the International Museum, fairly limited in its collection. Though Revolutionary exhibit was a fascinating collection of newspaper clippings, photographs and artifacts from the 1950's.

One of the highlights of my journey was a visit to Hemingway's house, located nine miles from Havana in a small suburb called San Francisco de Paula. Hemingway purchased the home in 1940 and lived there for twenty years. Surrounded by tropical fruit trees and palm trees, the house is stunning. Over 40,000 people visit the house every year and everything remains pretty much as he left it. On the bathroom wall remains the scribbles where he recorded his daily weight. And his typewriter sits at his desk. I was enthralled.

The bubble of the magic can pop pretty quickly in Cuba. On a Sunday morning I was strolling Havana's main street, where an exhibit of primitive art was on display at very reasonable prices. While examining a wooden sculpture of a hand holding a rose, a young man drifted into my space and asked me where I was from. The conversation continued for a few minutes about his struggle

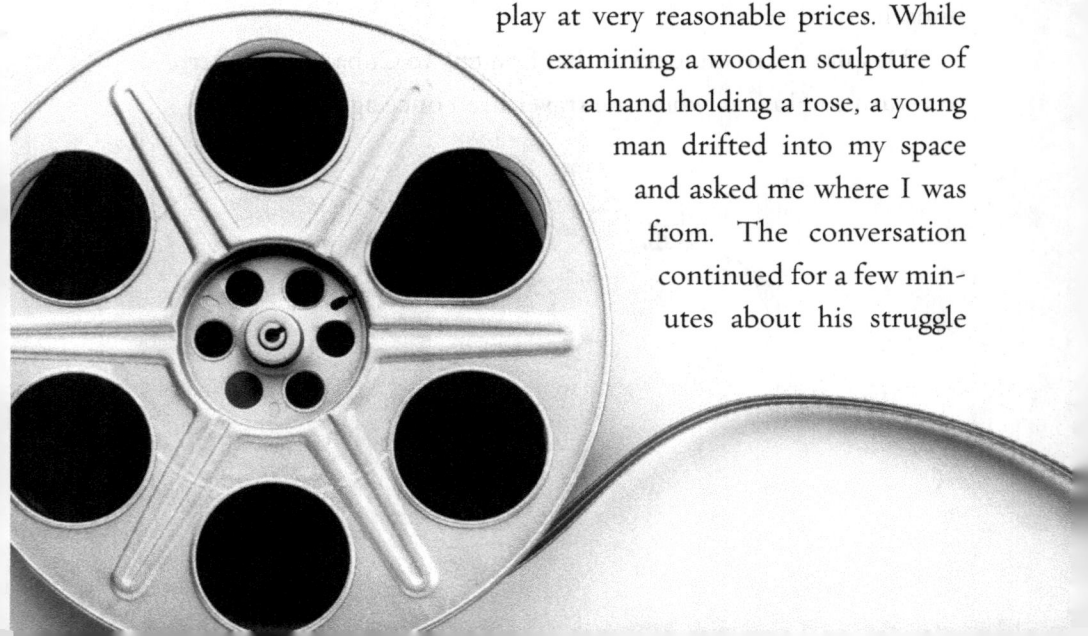

when out of nowhere four policemen surrounded us. They asked him for his ID and politely dismissed me. They took him into a car and disappeared. I witnessed first hand the experience of freedom lost.

When I returned to my hotel, I related the incident to the concierge and she proudly explained, "Oh yes, there are cameras everywhere on the streets, even in the trees and when the police who are monitoring the screens see a Cuban talking with a tourist they inform the police and they proceed to investigate."

"You don't have much freedom here do you?" I responded.

"This is Cuba, not America, we have rules sir," she said feeling empowered.

I simply shut up when I realized there might have been cameras around capturing that conversation.

Cuba's cuisine unlike its people was not known for being seductive, it lacked quality, imagination. But I heard that many new restaurants had popped up since I was last there. So I explored a number of them and happily realized a change had definitely taken place. The food was delicious and innovative. No longer were the vegetables canned. They were freshly served with a great variety of main courses influenced by its many European visitors. The seafood fresh, the lamb and octopus were the best I'd tasted anywhere. The atmosphere was full of chatty foreigners with no Americans in sight.

It was a major improvement since my last encounter, especially La Guarida restaurant, whose atmosphere and unique food excelled in Havana, and it was there where I discovered the seed for this book. The name means a den, a hideout, a

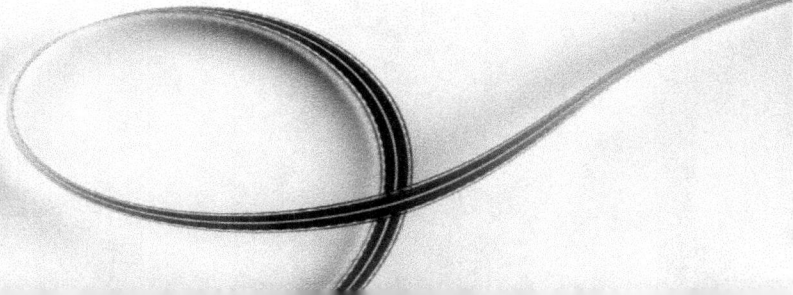

Entrance to La Guarida.

haunt or shelter. With its eclectic atmosphere, it sits enclosed on the third floor of a classical building that looks like it could collapse, making it decadently beautiful. But inside its colored walls they serve you and seduce you by the aromas of its fine food, where all the senses come together. Their challenge in the culinary aspect was trying to modernize the Cuban traditional kitchen, which they have done successfully.

As I was being escorted to my table, I noticed photographs of celebrities on the wall. There was Madonna, Sting, Beyonce, Jack Nicholson, Spielberg and many others. As I walked away, I

heard myself saying, "These are all celebrities who seduce, who come here to be seduced." So while sitting in this sexy ambience, I said to myself, "Seducing celebrities, with one meal at a time, that's what they do here. That's what I was doing there, being seduced."

I picked up the menu and ordered. The lobster tail was perfectly executed and so was the dessert, a three-milk-chocolate mousse cake.

I left the restaurant in bliss and walked safely back to my hotel.

My stay was cut short as a hurricane was blowing through in the next few days. I had experienced this the last time I was here, so I decided not to wait for another round of vengeance. As I was leaving for the airport, I had the realization that no matter how suppressed this society was, its love of music and passion for life, no matter how poor, resonated with joy in its struggle for freedom.

Arriving at the airport, I had packed in my bag a painting I purchased at a Sunday fair and attached with it the necessary documents to legally take it out of the country. As I boarded and sat in my seat my name was called to exit the plane to be questioned by authorities.

"What now?" I thought.

The hair rose on my arms. I was told to follow two guards down the bleak olive green stairs, all the while thinking I was about to see a communist country in action behind closed doors. It was simultaneously intriguing and frightening.

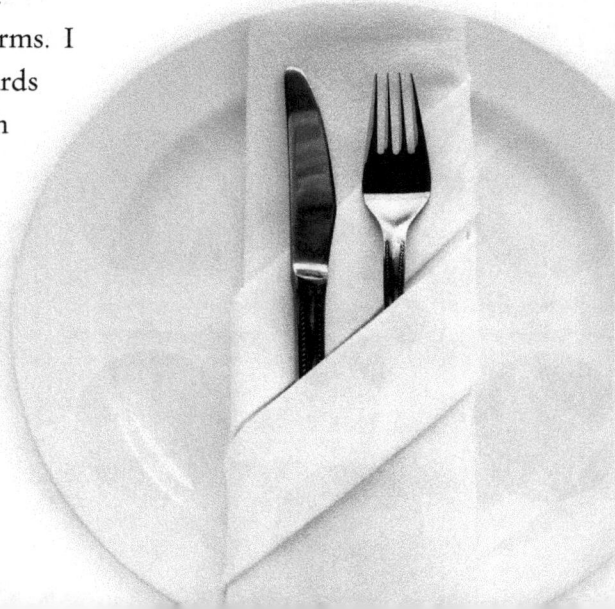

I was escorted into a dungeon-like room where a middle-aged woman in fatigues stood and proceeded to confront me. My bag was sitting on a table. She demanded my passport. As I handed it over a twenty-dollar bill fell out. Somehow, it had accidently gotten into my passport and by the expression on her face she clearly thought it was a bribe.

"Take that out of my sight," she said with disgust.

"Sorry, wrong person," I said, jokingly.

Sadly, she had no sense of humor. She stared back at me with disdain.

"This is serious. You think you can come to my country and steal our art? Open your bag," she demanded.

I was stunned. Obviously they had x-rayed my bag thinking the painting I had packed was a stolen masterpiece. I was slightly amused by the thought but her tough demeanor wiped the smirk off my face. The actor in me went into survival mode, and I calmly unzipped my bag. She rolled opened my painting when an expression of shock crossed her severe face. It was a humorous painting that reminded me of the artist "Botero," where a large woman, bent over with an exposed bum taunted a bunch of midget men with erections.

"That's it?" she said, clearly flabbergasted.

"Yes," I said. "What, you don't like my taste?"

"That's it?" she repeated again.

Game over.

Suddenly, I heard an announcement that my

Here we are entering La Guarida Restaurant in Havana.

plane was about to close its door. Irritated, she dismissed me, and I quickly rolled up my fake masterpiece into my bag and raced up the stairs. I made it in by seconds and breathed a sigh of relief as I sat in my seat.

I realized that in today's world the door that you passed through into a foreign landscape doesn't always guarantee it will be as easily opened to you on your way out. My motto: Always be prepared for the unexpected.

As my thoughts reflected back to my experiences in a land where change seemed to have been frozen since the 50's, wonderful and charming as it was, I looked forward to going home to the U.S. in the present.

But Cuba, you never disappoint. Besides a new book was forming in my mind...

"Seducing Celebrities, One Meal at a Time."

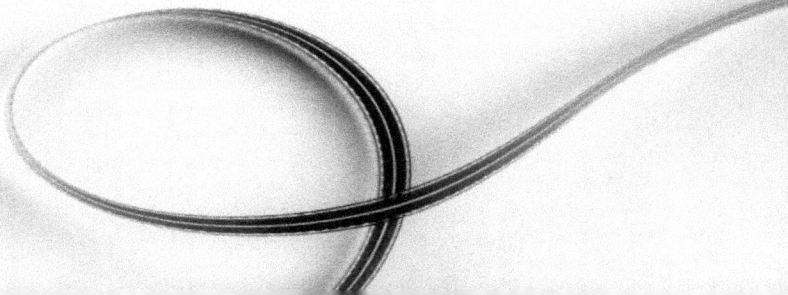

ABOUT THE AUTHOR

THAAO PENGHLIS was born and raised in Sydney, Australia to Greek-born parents. In 2015, Thaao was contracted to resume his most enduring character for NBC in *Days of Our Lives*, and then went on to star in the films *Slow Dancing in the Big City*, *Altered States*, *The Mirror* and *The Bell Jar*. Daytime audiences were first introduced to Penghlis in *General Hospital*. He also starred in the primetime series revival of *Mission Impossible*, which went on to be one of the most successful film franchises in history, with Tom Cruise. He starred in the mini-series *Sadat*, with Omar Sharif in *Memories of Midnight* and starred in the critically acclaimed television film *Under Siege* with Hal Holbrook for NBC. When he is off the stage, he is an intrepid world traveler, a gifted chef and a master storyteller.

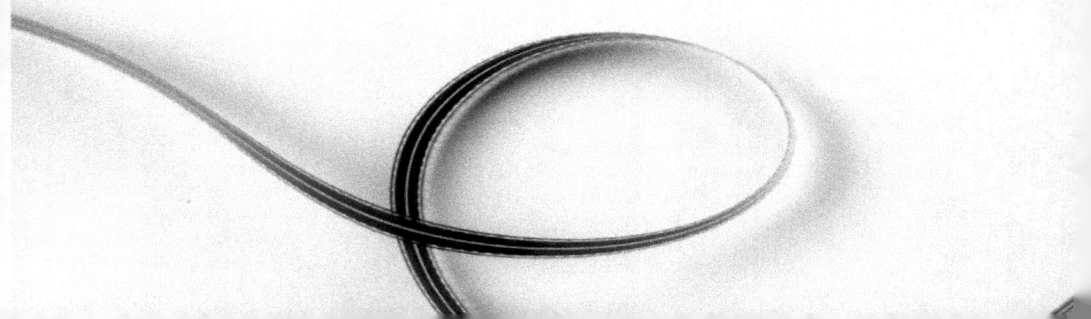

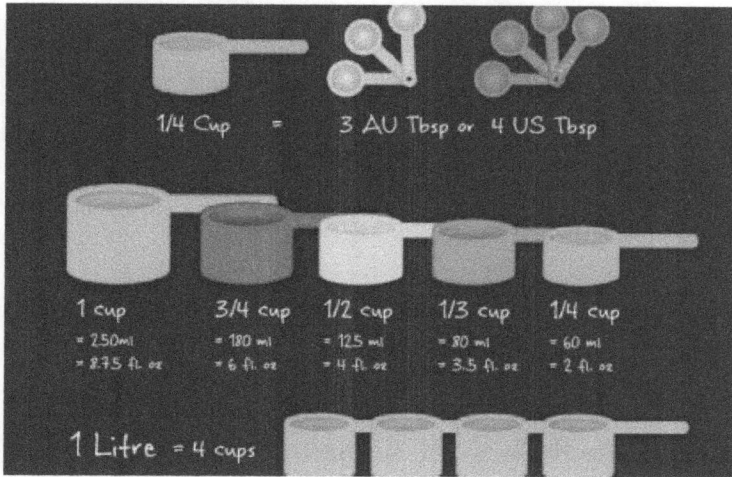

1/4 Cup = 3 AU Tbsp or 4 US Tbsp

1 cup	3/4 cup	1/2 cup	1/3 cup	1/4 cup
= 250ml	= 180 ml	= 125 ml	= 80 ml	= 60 ml
= 8.75 fl. oz	= 6 fl. oz	= 4 fl. oz	= 3.5 fl. oz	= 2 fl. oz

1 Litre = 4 cups

For sales, editorial information, subsidiary rights information
or a catalog, please write or phone or e-mail:

Brick Tower Press
Manhanset House
Dering Harbor, New York 11965-0342

Tel: 212-427-7139
www.BrickTowerPress.com
email: bricktower@aol.com

www.ingramcontent.com

For sales in the UK and Europe please contact our distributor,
Gazelle Book Services
White Cross Mills
Lancaster, LA1 4XS, UK
Tel: (01524) 68765 Fax: (01524) 63232
email: jacky@gazellebooks.co.uk

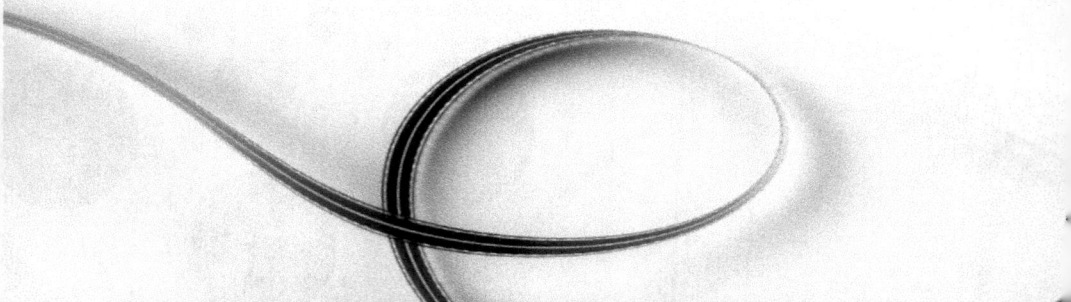